RUTH

More Than a Love Story

RUTH

{ *More Than a Love Story* }

Elizabeth Ahlman

CONCORDIA PUBLISHING HOUSE · SAINT LOUIS

Published by Concordia Publishing House
3558 S. Jefferson Avenue, St. Louis, MO 63118-3968
1-800-325-3040 · www.cph.org

Manufactured in the United States of America

2 3 4 5 6 7 8 9 10   23 22 21 20 19

TO MY WONDERFUL FAMILY, especially my mom, Pam Meckler; my husband, Christopher; and my sons, Thomas and Matthias. Thank you for always encouraging, helping, loving, and understanding. I love you all so much!

TO THE MONDAY MORNINGS FOR MOMS GROUP OF TRINITY LUTHERAN CHURCH, ELKHART, INDIANA: Thank you for your interest, your excitement, your faith, your love, and all of your Mommy advice! This book would not have been possible without the year I spent "teaching" all of you.

Table of Contents

FOREWORD

Why a New Study on Ruth?

IT WAS AS A FIRST YEAR DEACONESS student at Concordia Seminary, St. Louis, that I began working on Ruth as a Bible study. I was asked to teach a women's Bible study at my assigned fieldwork church. I picked Ruth because it was about a woman—or so I thought. I did the research, wrote the study, and taught it. Things went pretty well.

During my second year as a deaconess student, I was assigned to fieldwork in a federal prison, and I was again asked to present a Bible study. Since my classes were demanding, I went back to Ruth and material I had already prepared. I tweaked it a bit for the women of the prison. They had a lot to share and offer as we studied Ruth together. We had lively discussions, and I gained some insights.

As I wrapped up my graduate degree, I found that I had learned a great deal since writing the original material. In the meantime, an excellent *Concordia Commentary* on Ruth was published, and I began reading materials for my Master of Arts exam. When I returned to Ruth as a deaconess intern at Trinity Lutheran Church in Elkhart, Indiana, I knew there was so much more to Ruth than meets the eye at first, second, and even third glance. I rewrote my Bible study again and shared it with the Monday Mornings for Moms group. Even now, as I turn what was a Bible study outline into a real book, I am learning more, tweaking more, and being formed more by Ruth, because that is what Scripture does. It constantly renews, forms, enlightens, and especially evangelizes (that is, does the Gospel to us) no matter how many times we read the same passage.

A lot of studies of the Book of Ruth, including my own first attempts, are stuck in the quagmire of sentimental feelings about Ruth's words to Naomi in chapter 1 ("Where you go I will go, and where you lodge I will lodge"). Those words are used in marriage ceremonies, and while this is a fine use, it can lead to sentimentalizing and separating them from the context in which they were spoken. People worry over the nighttime visit scene in chapter 3, and scandalous or silly things are written about it. Some studies miss the mark because they either look at how we should be like Ruth or hijack the Book of Ruth into a chance to know more about how to be a "good Christian woman."

So, why a new study on Ruth? Because it has so much more to say than you or I may have thought. Because *Yahweh* has so much more to say through Ruth. Ruth isn't about you. It isn't about me. It isn't about how to be a better woman or about marriage relationships.

I hope that as you read this book, you will also be formed, renewed, enlightened, and evangelized, no matter how many times you've read the Book of Ruth in the past. Hopefully, this Bible study will point you to the deeper truths embedded in the historical narrative of Ruth's life, truths that reveal how God in Christ loves you and cares for you. I also hope that the amazing intricacy of God's Word, its literary prowess, and its connections would make you stop and say, "Wow!" So that you can have more "wow" moments in all of your reading, I wrote the study in a way that should allow you to gain further tools for reading.

To that end, I've chosen not just to share with you what the Book of Ruth says, but how it says it, from literary technique to closer looks at the Hebrew language. While I do quote mainly from the English Standard Version (ESV), I also at times refer to my own translations of Ruth. This is because, while the ESV does one of the most effective jobs of translating the Hebrew and Greek of the Bible, sometimes the language has more depth than can be understood from one English word. Therefore, at times I mention other ways of understanding certain words to offer a bigger picture of what the Hebrew language is conveying. I hope that you also find this to be helpful and interesting. In the end, I pray that you will walk away understanding more about how to read the Bible for all it is worth, and—most of all—I want you to walk away knowing what the Book of Ruth is really all about.

Ruth is about Jesus. It's about God. It's about salvation. Oh yes, this little book is bigger than you thought.

KEY TERMS AND CONCEPTS

ANALOGICAL PROPHECY: Analogical prophecy prophesies about Christ by way of analogy. An analogy is a comparison of two things with similar features that shows how the two things are related. In analogical prophecy, two events (or items) are compared, and the similarities uncovered by the comparison show how the first event prophesied the second. For instance, Noah and his family being preserved on the ark can be seen as an analogical prophecy of Baptism. They were saved through water. Peter makes this connection in 1 Peter 3:18–22:

> For Christ also suffered once for sins, the righteous for the unrighteous, that He might bring us to God, being put to death in the flesh but made alive in the spirit, in which He went and proclaimed to the spirits in prison, because they formerly did not obey, when God's patience waited in the days of Noah, while the ark was being prepared, in which a few, that is, eight persons, were brought safely through water. Baptism, which corresponds to this, now saves you, not as a removal of dirt from the body but as an appeal to God for a good conscience, through the resurrection of Jesus Christ, who has gone into heaven and is at the right hand of God, with angels, authorities, and powers having been subjected to Him.

In this way, the flood is both a historical event that displays God at work in His creation for the sake of His people and an event that prophesies about how God will work in the future to save His people through Baptism. (Analogical prophecy usually refers to events or things, while typology refers to people from the Old Testament as prophecies of Christ. See below for the discussion on typology.)

CHESED: The Hebrew word *chesed* is rich in meaning and often not translated well into English. It can mean loving-kindness, faithfulness, and steadfast love. In all its meanings, this word goes beyond the human ability to show loving-kindness or faithfulness. It means an enduring faithfulness, a saving loving-kindness. *Chesed* is, ultimately, a defining characteristic of Yahweh. It is best understood for the purposes of Ruth as Yahweh's faithfulness to His covenant with His people—His covenant to bring about their salvation.

CHIASM: The term *chiasm* is derived from the Greek letter *chi* (X) and can be diagrammed like the Greek letter *chi*. A chiasm occurs when a section of text has similar parts at the beginning and end that mirror each other. Often there is also a central portion called the *fulcrum*. In other words, there are similar clauses at the beginning and end of the text that act like bookends. The central portion is emphasized by the chiastic structure. Chiasms are often diagrammed using the markers A, A', B, B', C, C' and so on (or using numerals where I have apostrophes). A chiasm can occur over one or two sentences or over larger portions of text. Psalm 51:1 is a good example of a simple chiasm with no fulcrum:

> **A** "Have mercy on me, O God,
>> **B** according to Your steadfast love;
>> **B'** according to Your abundant mercy
> **A'** blot out my transgressions."[1]

A chiastic structure adds emphasis to what is being said and reinforces main ideas. When there is a fulcrum, the chiastic structure makes the central point pop out at the reader.

CHRISTOCENTRIC: This term is used as a way of saying that a particular text, and indeed the Bible as a whole, is centered in Christ. In other words, the Scriptures always have Jesus Christ and His salvific work as their central theme and unifying element.

CHRISTOTELIC: *Telic* means "end." This term expresses the truth that the end goal and ultimate aim of all the Holy Scriptures is Jesus Christ. All Scripture finds its fulfillment, full meaning, full expression, and full purpose in Jesus. The true reason behind the Scriptures is to reveal Jesus Christ, the Son of God, who died for the sins of sinful humanity.

---

1   This example is taken from Michael J. Gorman, *Elements of Biblical Exegesis: A Basic Guide for Students and Ministers.* (Peabody, MA: Hendrickson Publishers, 2001), 82.

HEBREW BIBLE: The Hebrew Bible is arranged differently than English editions. The Hebrew Bible is arranged into three categories: the Torah, the Writings, and the Prophets. Ruth is considered a writing. Below are examples of what make up the three categories in the Hebrew Bible:

Torah: *Torah* means "law." The Torah is made up of Genesis, Exodus, Leviticus, Numbers, and Deuteronomy.

Writings: Ruth, Job, 1 and 2 Samuel, 1 and 2 Kings, 1 and 2 Chronicles, Psalms, Proverbs, and such

Prophets: Jonah, Nehemiah, Jeremiah, Nahum, Habakkuk, Isaiah, and all of the other major and minor prophets. In English editions, the books of the Bible are arranged chronologically. Since the events in the Book of Ruth occur during the time of Judges, English Bibles place Ruth after the Book of Judges. In the Hebrew Bible, Ruth follows Proverbs, which is important to the interpretation of Ruth since the final section of Proverbs is on the Worthy Woman, and Ruth has many of the characteristics described in Proverbs 31:10–31.

INCLUSIO: A literary device by which a section of text is bracketed in order to emphasize the meaning of that section, an inclusio is formed when the same word or phrase is used to both begin and end a section of text. By placing the same word or phrase at both the beginning and the end, the narrator signals that the intervening verses or words are to be closely interpreted and inform one another. The word or phrase that is used is a key to the meaning of that section as a whole. There are several inclusios in Ruth.

LEITWORT: A *leitwort* is a key word (or phrase) that is repeated throughout a section of Scripture. A *leitwort* includes different forms of the same word, such as justify, justification, justified, and unjust. It is important to pay close attention whenever a word is repeated in a given section of Scripture. The meaning, theme, or motif is tied to the function of the word in that section.

MERISM: Merism is a poetic device used often in Hebrew that gives two opposite ideas or items and includes everything in between. Merism occurs in Ruth's speech to Naomi in the first chapter. Another example is found in Genesis 8:22, where one of the merisms is seedtime and harvest. By listing the opposite ends of the process of cultivation, the Lord also includes in His promise every step that comes in between. Also covered, then, are the times when the seed sprouts, the roots burrow into the ground, the first shoot pushes out of the earth, the bud flowers, and so forth. Perhaps the most familiar example of merism is when Jesus calls Himself the "Alpha and the Omega," (the beginning and the end) (Revelation 1:8). He is not just these two things, but all that comes between. In other words, Jesus is everything.

MICROCOSM: A microcosm reflects larger realities in a much smaller form. In literature, microcosm is used to make a point about or highlight characteristics of the larger world or reality. Take for instance the novel *The Lord of the Flies* by William Golding. The story is about a group of boys and takes place on a small island, a microcosm that reflects on the larger world beyond the story, society as a whole. As the boys are alone on the island trying to figure out how to live—some trying for a more civilized existence while others become amoral and brutal—Golding is making a commentary on the overall struggles in human society between these two possibilities. The smaller world created by Golding reflects on and interprets the larger world we live in. The boys on the island are a microcosm of all human society. Ruth is a biblical example of a microcosm. This will be explained in the study.

NARRATIVE: The term narrative refers in general to a story that is told through narration (description) and dialogue. Narratives can be either nonfiction (true stories) or fiction. Narrative is often used to mean nonfiction writing, as in writing about a specific event in one's own life (memoir as opposed to short story). A narrative contains people, places, events, dialogue, description, and more. Narrative is used frequently in the Scriptures, especially in the Old Testament, to relate historical events and personages. For example, Genesis is a series of short narratives beginning with Adam and Eve and progressing to

Joseph. Judges, different than Genesis in its themes and theological motives as well as in its scope, is a narrative relating an overall history of Israel between the exodus and the establishment of the kingship. The larger narrative of Judges is made up of shorter narratives concerning specific persons and specific times in that span.

A narrative structure allows for creativity in how the history is related while still allowing all things to be historically accurate. It is important to remember and understand that creativity does not equal falseness or unreliability. God Himself chose this medium to make the history of His work in the world coherent, comprehensible, rich, and Christ-centered. Creative forms of writing, such as narrative or poetry, allow for important theological truths to be highlighted or to come through clearly. The first few chapters of Genesis concerning Adam and Eve, for instance, are a true narrative of God's creation of the world and of the first humans. However, they are also narratives that, through their artistry and beauty, tell important truths concerning ourselves, our natures, and how God ordered this world.

Genesis gives us two depictions of Yahweh's activity of creating. The first is an overview from God's perspective in which the literary and narrative device *leitwort* offers an interpretive tool that helps us understand that all of what God created is good and that man is the crowning achievement of that creation. The second chapter of Genesis then reviews the creation from a view closer to how mankind sees it. By using further details and description, the narrator focuses on important aspects of creation that point to several theological truths, such as the order of creation, God's design for marriage, headship, original sin, and our responsibility to care for creation (dominion).

REMNANT THEOLOGY: Remnant theology refers to a theme throughout the Old Testament in which God's people frequently fall away from Him but a small contingent always remains faithful. Yahweh repeatedly says that He will prosper and grow this remnant, using it to bring about His chosen Servant. The remnant theme occurs early and frequently. For instance, in Exodus 32, the people worship the golden calf, but some do not participate (see especially Exodus 32:26–29). The

Lord sends the Levites through the tribes and three thousand people die. Those who are left are the remnant that believes. Similarly, in 1 Kings 19, after he kills the false prophets and his life is threatened by Jezebel, Elijah believes that he is the only faithful one left in all of Israel. Yahweh corrects him:

> [Elijah] said, "I have been very jealous for the LORD, the God of hosts. For the people of Israel have forsaken Your covenant, thrown down Your altars, and killed Your prophets with the sword, and I, even I only, am left, and they seek my life, to take it away." And the LORD said to him, "Go, return on your way to the wilderness of Damascus. And when you arrive, you shall anoint Hazael to be king over Syria. And Jehu the son of Nimshi you shall anoint to be king over Israel, and Elisha the son of Shaphat of Abel-meholah you shall anoint to be prophet in your place. And the one who escapes from the sword of Hazael shall Jehu put to death, and the one who escapes from the sword of Jehu shall Elisha put to death. Yet I will leave seven thousand in Israel, all the knees that have not bowed to Baal, and every mouth that has not kissed him." (1 Kings 19:14–18)

Notice that there are seven thousand in Israel that Yahweh will "leave." These are the remnant of faithful believers. Out of them, God will continue to keep for Himself a covenant people who are inheritors of the promise made to Adam, Eve, Abraham, and Sarah.

This theme is also very strong in Isaiah. Here is an example from Isaiah 10 about the return of the faithful remnant to Israel and out of their captivity:

> In that day the remnant of Israel and the survivors of the house of Jacob will no more lean on him who struck them, but will lean on the LORD, the Holy One of Israel, in truth. A remnant will return, the remnant of Jacob, to the mighty God. For though your people Israel be as the sand of the sea, only a remnant of them will return. Destruction is decreed, overflowing with righteousness. (Isaiah 10:20–22)

Here Isaiah records God's words concerning Israel's captivity and Assyria. There will be a remnant, but it will be only a few compared to how many there were before. This theme continues in other portions of Scripture as well. The remnant is the faithful who believe in God.

He always rescues them, brings them to Himself, and preserves them so that the salvation for all people will come from their midst.

TYPOLOGY: The study of how Jesus is foreshadowed by certain persons in the Old Testament is called typology; these people are called "types of Christ." A type of Christ foreshadows Jesus by his characteristics, his actions, and how God views him. David is a type of Christ, as well. One way is that he is a king, whereas Christ is the perfect, eternal King. Several other Old Testament persons are types of Christ, and some of them will be examined in this study and in the Answer Key (page 171). Through their lives, characteristics, and actions, these people point us forward to Jesus Christ, who became the perfect and ultimate Prophet, Priest, King, Son of God, and sacrifice.

YAHWEH: God's proper name, as revealed to Moses in Exodus 3, is Yahweh. God gives His name, Yahweh, to His people. It is a wonderful gift that shows who belongs among God's chosen people. Yahweh is the word that actually appears in the Hebrew text wherever our English translation gives us "Lord." In Hebrew, all words are made up of consonants that are written letters or characters. Before the intertestamental period, only the consonants were written. During the intertestamental period, the Masoretes—Jewish scribes—inserted vowels by "pointing" each word, that is placing dashes and periods under the consonants to create the full word. There were strict regulations for the use of God's name, so that no one would even accidentally take His name in vain, so the Masoretes pointed the consonants in the name of God with the vowels for the Hebrew word Adonai, which simply means "Lord." The four Hebrew letters for God's name are hwhy and are transliterated as YHWH. When the Jewish reader came to YHWH, the pointing under the letters reminded the reader to speak "Adonai." This was not understood for many years by translators, who translated the consonants YHWH with the vowel pointing for Adonai as "Jehovah." This was incorrect.

Yahweh can also mean "I am." When Jesus refers to Himself this way in the Gospel of John, He is identifying Himself as Yahweh, the one true God. This is why the Pharisees, Sadducees, lawyers, and priests were so shocked. They believed He was blaspheming by using God's name and by claiming to be God. As redeemed people who live in Christ, we can freely use God's special revealed name to praise, petition, and proclaim Him to others. It is the name that Ruth and Boaz used. Therefore, *Yahweh* is used frequently in this study.

CHAPTER 1

RUTH 1:1-5:
SETTING THE SCENE

OPENING PRAYER: LORD JESUS CHRIST, You are
the Word made flesh. Reveal Yourself to us through Your
Word so that we may know You and cling to You through all
trials and temptations, for You live and reign with the Father
and the Holy Spirit, one God, now and forever. Amen.

AS WITH EVERY BIBLICAL BOOK, it is important to understand some
background of the Book of Ruth in order to place it into the context of
history and the canonical Scriptures as a whole, and to properly interpret it in line with the *regula fidei,* or the rule of faith. The *regula fidei*
is reflected in the creeds (the Apostles' Creed, the Athanasian Creed,
and the Nicene Creed). The *regula fidei* shapes our understanding of
Scripture by pointing us to the central truths of the Bible and guiding
our interpretation of it. If a particular interpretation runs counter to
something we read in the creeds, then that interpretation is at best sus-
pect and at worst heretical. Even the interpretation of a book such as
Ruth should have at its center Christ and Him crucified, in accord with
the *regula fidei* and the creeds the Church has confessed for centuries.

Ruth as a whole is different from most of the other books of the
Bible with the exception, perhaps, of Esther. Ruth is a focused narrative in that it looks at a specific group of people in the history of the
people of God. Unlike the sweeping narratives of Genesis or Exodus,
which cover a lot of ground and time, Ruth narrows in on a small
group of people and a sliver of time in history. At first glance, it seems a
quaint tale about a faithful daughter-in-law, a bitter mother-in-law, romantic love, and a baby. Against the backdrop of Genesis and Exodus,
it seems a bit odd and out of place. Yet Ruth builds on many themes
in the Old Testament, and its narrow narrative focus is important to

understanding how to interpret the book as a whole. In building on those themes and understanding of Ruth, we find that this little book that seems so preoccupied with three people (Ruth, Naomi, and Boaz) in fact impacts many more than just those three. Therefore, we will start by considering the context of the Book of Ruth.

RUTH'S PLACE IN THE CANON

When the Hebrew canon was first being formed, it was divided into three groupings (this is still how the Hebrew Bible is often divided). These groupings are usually the Torah, the Writings, and the Prophets.

The *Torah* is comprised of the first five books of the Bible (Genesis, Exodus, Leviticus, Numbers, and Deuteronomy). The *Writings* is a catch-all category for many different types of writings such as the Psalms, Proverbs, Ruth, Esther, and others. The *Prophets* refers to the books written by the prophets such as Isaiah, Kings, Chronicles, and Jeremiah. In the Hebrew Bible, Ruth was placed after Proverbs and before Song of Solomon. Following directly on the heels of Proverbs 31, Ruth is closely connected to it (more on this in chapter 5). This close connection between the woman of Proverbs 31 and Ruth seems to be why the Book of Ruth followed the Book of Proverbs in the Hebrew canon.

The Old Testament Books According to Type

TORAH	WRITINGS/WISDOM	PROPHETS
Genesis	Psalms	Joshua
Exodus	Job	Judges
Leviticus	Proverbs	Samuel
Numbers	Ruth	Kings
Deuteronomy	Song of Songs	Isaiah
	Ecclesiastes	Jeremiah
	Lamentations	Ezekiel
	Esther	Hosea
	Daniel	Joel
	Ezra	Amos
	Nehemiah	Obadiah
	Chronicles	Micah
		Nahum
		Habakkuk
		Zephaniah
		Zechariah
		Haggai

Genesis	Nahum
Exodus	Habakkuk
Leviticus	Zephaniah
Numbers	Haggai
Deuteronomy	Zechariah
Joshua	Malachi
Judges	Psalms
Samuel	Job
Kings	Proverbs
Isaiah	Ruth
Jeremiah	Song of Songs
Ezekiel	Ecclesiastes
Hosea	Lamentations
Joel	Esther
Amos	Daniel
Obadiah	Ezra
Jonah	Nehemiah
Micah	Chronicles

In our Christian Bible, the books of the Old Testament are grouped more or less chronologically. The first five books are in the same order as in the Hebrew canon, or the Torah. However, in most English translations of the Bible, Ruth follows the Book of Judges, because it is closely related to the time of the judges, chronologically speaking. The tradition of placing Ruth after Judges began with the Septuagint, a Greek translation of the Hebrew Old Testament from about the second century BC. It was present in this form before Jesus' time. Both placements of Ruth are helpful to interpretation of the book, its setting, theology, and connectedness to other parts of Scripture.[2]

TYPE OF LITERATURE

The Bible is a literary masterpiece. Please do not panic at the word *literary*. *Literature/literary* does not equal *fiction*. Literature, good literature, can come either in the fiction or the nonfiction variety; it can even come as sacred writings. One of the most wonderful aspects

---

2   For more on the formation of the Old Testament canon, see Andrew Steinmann, *The Oracles of God: The Old Testament Canon*, (St. Louis: Concordia Academic Press, 1999).

of the Bible is the fact of its beauty, depth, and variety as a literary masterpiece. The beauty of the scriptural writings, as well as their interconnectedness, serves to better show us Christ and Him crucified. The creativity and historical accuracy of all Scripture serve to show Christ clearly. As a literary masterpiece, the Bible is made up of different types of literature, including prophetic, apocalyptic, narrative, and wisdom literature. In order to properly interpret a specific book—or even a passage of Scripture—it is important to understand what type of literature it is and how that affects the way we understand it.

Ruth is a narrative, a true account of real events told in a story form with one or more main themes as its goal. This is similar to any personal narrative one might tell about a life event of one's own. Biblical narratives are just what we would expect from a narrative with plot, characters, arc, conflict, and resolution. They tell the story through description and through dialogue. However, narratives in the Bible are not just stories; they are historical fact that reveals the work of God in the world on behalf of His people and that ultimately prophesies about Christ analogically. In other words, biblical narratives prophesy about Christ through analogy to historic events. This means that something in each narrative is similar to something that occurs in the life of Christ and can be understood to be a prophecy about a certain aspect of Christ's life, death, resurrection, or work on our behalf. For instance, in Numbers, Moses is instructed to lift up the bronze serpent (Numbers 21:4–9) after the Israelites are bitten by fiery serpents sent by Yahweh to punish them for speaking against Yahweh. All those who look upon the serpent live, while all those who do not die. We see this event as an analogy of the crucifixion of Christ. Christ is the "bronze serpent" who was lifted up upon the cross. All those who look in faith and by faith on Christ the crucified will live and will not perish from the bite of sin, death, and the devil. In this way, not only do we have the historical account of Yahweh's work on behalf of the Israelites at the time of the exodus, but we also see how all of Scripture ultimately points us toward Christ and is Christ-centered, just as Christ demonstrated to His apostles on the road to Emmaus (Luke 24).

Analogy and Typology: The Scriptures often point to Christ through two literary means: analogy and typology. As discussed, the Scriptures can prophesy about Christ by way of analogy with regard to events. For instance, the event of the flood foreshadows and points toward Baptism and how God uses Baptism to drown our sinful flesh and raise us to new life. On the other hand, typology usually occurs when a person in the Old Testament can be likened to Christ in such a way that that person foreshadows the Greater One to come. A good example of this is Moses, a prophet who is called humble or meek (Numbers 12:3) and who speaks to God (Numbers 3:7–8). These are just a couple of characteristics that make Moses a type of Jesus. However, Moses is still a flawed human being. Jesus is all that Moses is and more, but where Moses is imperfect because of sin, Jesus is perfect. Jesus is God's greatest prophet, He is the most humble man on earth, He speaks to God face-to-face, and He is without sin. For more on Moses as a type, see the answer key. Elements of Ruth prophesy Christ both analogically and typologically.

TIME IN WHICH THE STORY IS SET

Ruth 1:1 states, "In the days when the judges ruled there was a famine in the land, and a man of Bethlehem in Judah went to sojourn in the country of Moab, he and his wife and his two sons." From this sentence, we understand that the events that occur in the Book of Ruth happened during the period of the judges. The time of the judges was approximately 1380–1050 BC. This was the intermediary period in the Israelites' history, after the conquest of the land (as recorded in Joshua) and before God chose to give them the monarchy (see 1 Samuel 8–10). The judges were typically lay people raised up by God to help rule the people, especially during times of crisis; their duties were not generally religious in nature. This period was a difficult one in the lives of God's people, because they had failed to drive out all the inhabitants of the land, refused God's rule and gifts, and intermarried with the people of the land, which often led to idolatry by the Israelites. Ruth may have taken place during the events recorded in Judges 6. We will return to this hypothesis as we go through Ruth.

TIME OF COMPOSITION

There are two schools of thought about the time Ruth was written. The first is the later date, which used to be the favored viewpoint. For a time, scholars believed Ruth to have been written some time after the exile (Babylonian exile, 586/7–515/10 BC). This was put forward in part by form critics, whose interpretive lens was an offshoot of historical criticism. These scholars deal with the biblical text without the assumptions that we as Lutheran Christians hold: that the Scriptures are God-breathed and true. They posited that the book was written at such a late date merely as a tale to help combat Ezra and Nehemiah's rules concerning marriage to foreigners. Their theories are not solidly based on the text itself, an honest interpretation of Scripture, or even archaeological evidence.[3] But the majority of scholars no longer believe this to be correct. Today's conservative scholars now favor the early date, and that time frame is the assumption of this study. Most now say that Ruth was penned prior to the Babylonian exile. In the *Concordia Commentary* on Ruth, John R. Wilch concludes that Ruth was written during the latter half of David's reign, during the period of the united monarchy. This would place the time of writing sometime between 1005 and 985 BC.[4] Wilch concludes this because of several factors, one of which is that the Book of Ruth includes the genealogy of David and touches on themes important to David's rule.

PURPOSE

The nature of biblical writing includes purposes that pertain to the immediate time period in which it was written. However, its theological purpose extends over time and beyond the more immediate scope of the writing itself. The purpose of Ruth in its time was to demonstrate the legitimacy of David's rule and his connection to Yahweh's work in the lives of Israel's ancestors.[5] Proving his legitimacy was important for David, because he was anointed by Samuel to be king when the succession should have gone to someone in Saul's family (see 1 Samuel 18– 2 Samuel 5, for example).[6] The Book of Ruth defends David by reciting the genealogy and capturing how it was that the line continued despite

---

[3] See Horace D. Hummel, *The Word Becoming Flesh: An Introduction to the Origin, Purpose, and Meaning of the Old Testament*, (St. Louis: Concordia Publishing House, 1979), 509–10; and John R. Wilch, Ruth, Concordia Commentary, ed. Christopher W. Mitchell (St. Louis: Concordia Publishing House, 2006), 15–16.

[4] Wilch, 16.

[5] Raymond B. Dillard & Tremper Longman III, *An Introduction to the Old Testament*, (Grand Rapids, MI: Zondervan, 1994), 131.

[6] Wilch, 24.

the deaths of Elimelech, Mahlon, and Chilion. It also defends David's practice of allowing believing foreigners to enter into the congregation of Israel. (Ruth, the person, is an excellent example of a believing foreigner.) The Book of Ruth also defends David's choice of a foreign wife by reporting that Boaz took Ruth, a believing foreigner, as his wife. The theological purpose of the Book of Ruth is to show God working in history to carry out His plan of salvation, which culminates in Christ Jesus.

In both purposes, God's activity on behalf of His people to care for and save them also proclaims God's saving activity to us today in our own situations and circumstances.

{ *David and Foreigners* }

David married a foreign wife and employed many foreigners, both individuals and groups, in his army. To some people of his day, that would have been problematic. David seems, however, to have only allowed those who converted to faith in Yahweh to remain in Jerusalem and be a part of the assembly. For example:

- David showed favor to the king of Moab by asking him to protect David's family (1 Samuel 22:3–5). It may also be that because Ruth was his ancestor, David chose the King of Moab as a person likely to help him protect his parents.
- David married a princess of the Aramean kingdom of Geshur, Maacah (2 Samuel 3:3).
- Ittai, a believing Philistine from Gath, fought with David. This episode is almost a replay of Ruth 1 (see 2 Samuel 15:13–23).
- Uriah the Hittite was a believing foreigner, as demonstrated by his loyalty to his fellow troops, to David, and to Yahweh when he makes a confession concerning the ark of the covenant (2 Samuel 11:1–11).

These few examples demonstrate David's close relationships with believing foreigners. The point, though, is that these people were believers. David was faithful to Yahweh as well, despite his many other flaws, and faithfulness, not ethnicity, was what mattered to him. It is safe to assume, however, that not all the Israelites would have agreed with foreigners being welcomed and trusted by their king (see 2 Samuel 5:1–10, where David allows the Jebusites to remain in Jerusalem, though they were among the seven nations that were supposed to be completely driven out of the Promised Land in Joshua 3:10). Yahweh had often spoken against mixing with foreigners and frequently commanded that all foreigners be put to death during wars, especially during the conquering of the land (see for instance Joshua 6:17–18, where only Rahab and her family are spared from the destruction of Jericho; Deuteronomy 7:1–2; Deuteronomy 20:16–17).[7]

IMPORTANT MOTIFS AND THEOLOGY

AS WE BEGIN TO DISCUSS THE BOOK of Ruth in depth, it is helpful to keep in mind some of its important motifs and theological implications. All of these will come to the forefront as we proceed.

MOTIFS:

- Emptiness and fulfillment
- Faithfulness
- Redemption
- The hidden God
- Honor
- Acceptance of foreigners[8]

THEOLOGY:

- Christotelic/Christology
- God's work behind the scenes
- Faith
- Human agency
- Sacrifice
- Substitution
- Redemption
- Suffering
- Witness[9]

---

7 See Wilch, 25–28. Wilch notes that while there is no direct reference to opposition to David due to the inclusion of foreigners, this is likely because the accounts written of him were sympathetic (see especially p. 28). However, many commentaries and other resources, including Wilch, assume this to be a problem for some. See also Dillard and Longman, 131, who also note that foreigners often made up a huge portion of David's power base, which would also make such a reference to a foreign relative who converted helpful for David. Also, given the Lord's commands concerning foreigners being barred from the assembly, it is safe to assume that some opposition would have been partly aroused by his favor to foreigners. Additionally, David faced many other rebellions and much opposition from those who supported Saul's line (especially those from the tribe of Benjamin, Saul's tribe) and those who coveted his throne (such as his son Absalom). For opposition to David's rule, see also 2 Samuel 2:8–11; 15; 16:5–14; 20.

8 Wilch 30–60.

9 Wilch 60–86.

Verse by Verse Analysis

READ RUTH 1:1–5

BIBLICAL NARRATIVE IS CONDUCTED MOSTLY through dialogue; therefore, it is important to note any time the narrator speaks. In these opening verses of the Book of Ruth, the narrator offers important information concerning the backdrop of the story to unlock the meaning of the dialogue that follows in the next section. The narrator shows how the next event that is recorded—Naomi's determination to return to Israel—came to be, and also sets up important theological background, as we will see later. The Hebrew narrator is always fully reliable and often guides the reader in interpretation by offering hints, such as special literary constructions and references to other Scriptures.

> **The Hebrew Narrator:** In terms of role and in the world of the story, the Hebrew narrator is omniscient but selective in what he reveals for the sake of artistry and meaning. He is always reliable and never misleads. The conceptual world of the Hebrew narrator is one in which man is created in the image of God but does not live up to that ethical standard. The Hebrew understanding of unity is different from our modern one. It holds things in tension, which is to us disjunctive (think of the two creation accounts or the two introductions of David in 1 Samuel). He often portrays the world through two different viewpoints:
>
> 1. Concise, symmetrically stylized vertical view— God to the world below, and
> 2. Human-centered, very detailed, horizontal view.

At the beginning, we are introduced to Naomi and Elimelech, who are married, and to their children, Mahlon and Chilion. The narrator also introduces us to the wives of Mahlon and Chilion: Ruth and Orpah, two Moabite women. Hebrew names have important meanings. *Elimelech* means "my God is King." Ideally, the person lives up to his or her name by, in this case, honoring God as King. *Naomi* means "pleasant, delightful." The meanings of the names of Mahlon and Chilion are uncertain, which suits the fact that they are marginalized in the Book of Ruth. It is not the men, but Naomi and Ruth who are most important and come to the forefront. Translation difficulties make the meanings of the names of both Orpah and Ruth uncertain. *The Lutheran Study Bible* notes that tradition links Ruth's name with the Hebrew word for "friend." However, Wilch compellingly argues that the most plausible meaning for *Ruth* comes from the root word meaning "be saturated, drink one's fill." For our purposes, therefore, her name means "saturation, a drink, refreshment, satiety, or fullness."[10]

The narrator also helps the reader understand the lineage of Elimelech and his family within the twelve tribes of Israel (descended from the twelve sons of Jacob). Each tribe was further divided into clans. Elimelech's family was part of the Ephrathite clan of the tribe of Judah. As a member of the tribes of Israel, Elimelech had a part in the inheritance of the land. Each tribe was assigned a portion of the Promised Land. Within the tribe, each clan had a separate portion. Those were then divided by household. Elimelech owned a plot of land out of his tribe and clan's allotment.

As part of his introduction, the narrator tells us the time in which the story is set. As noted above, Ruth is set during the time of Judges. Judges 6:1–10 reads:

> The people of Israel did what was evil in the sight of the LORD, and the LORD gave them into the hand of Midian seven years. And the hand of Midian overpowered Israel, and because of Midian the people of Israel made for themselves the dens that are in the mountains and the caves and the strongholds. For whenever the Israelites planted crops, the Midianites and the Amalekites and the people of the East would come up against them. They would encamp against them and devour the produce of the land, as far as Gaza, and leave no sustenance in Israel and no sheep or ox or donkey. For they would come up with their livestock and their tents; they would come like locusts in number—both they and their camels could not be counted—so that they laid waste the land as they came in. And Israel was brought very low because of Midian. And the people of Israel cried out for help to the LORD.

---

10   Wilch, 116. Wilch's argument is based on word studies linking it to what he thinks is the more plausible root Hebrew word. The tradition of "friend" comes from a Syriac translation and its equivalent Hebrew verb. In other words, they took the word used in Syriac and went backwards to say from what Hebrew word it would have been translated. The closest Hebrew root word means "saturate, water, cause to drink." Wilch explains the Hebrew conventions for giving the name of Ruth the feminine ending. Given that this corresponds extremely well to one of the main themes of Ruth, and combined with Wilch's excellent work on the linguistics, this meaning of Ruth will be preferred in our study.

When the people of Israel cried out to the LORD on account of the Midianites, the LORD sent a prophet to the people of Israel. And he said to them, "Thus says the LORD, the God of Israel: I led you up from Egypt and brought you out of the house of slavery. And I delivered you from the hand of the Egyptians and from the hand of all who oppressed you, and drove them out before you and gave you their land. And I said to you, 'I am the LORD your God; you shall not fear the gods of the Amorites in whose land you dwell.' But you have not obeyed My voice."

At this time in history, the people of Israel had again abandoned God and did "what was evil in the sight of [Yahweh]" (Judges 6:1). This cycle of the people sinning, Yahweh punishing them, the people crying out for help, and Yahweh rescuing them by raising up a judge recurs throughout the Book of Judges. It is symptomatic of the fact that the Israelites did not regard God as their King.

Given the extreme famine conditions described in Judges 6, many commentators suggest that Naomi and Elimelech left Israel for Moab during this particular famine. Such conditions may have driven some Israelites to leave the land God had given them to live among foreign, pagan people. However, our narrator focuses only on one specific family and their journey.

In the NIV, the verb is translated "went to live for a while," while the ESV translates it as "sojourn." *Sojourn* means to seek refuge and live somewhere as a stranger, usually temporarily, although a sojourner tends to stay a longer time than a regular visitor or a foreigner. *Sojourn* captures more of the sense of a journey and connects Naomi and Elimelech lexically with other famous biblical personages. Other biblical characters have also sojourned because of famine. Here are some examples:

- Abraham, Genesis 12:10: "Now there was a famine in the land. So Abram went down to Egypt to **sojourn** there, for the famine was severe in the land."
- Isaac, Genesis 26:1–3: "Now there was a famine in the land, besides the former famine that was in the days of Abraham. And Isaac went to Gerar to Abimelech king of the Philistines. And

the LORD appeared to him and said, 'Do not go down to Egypt; dwell in the land of which I shall tell you. **Sojourn** in this land, and I will be with you and will bless you, for to you and to your offspring I will give all these lands, and I will establish the oath that I swore to Abraham your father.'"

- Jacob and his sons, Genesis 47:1–4: "So Joseph went in and told Pharaoh, 'My father and my brothers, with their flocks and herds and all that they possess, have come from the land of Canaan. They are now in the land of Goshen.' And from among his brothers he took five men and presented them to Pharaoh. Pharaoh said to his brothers, 'What is your occupation?' And they said to Pharaoh, 'Your servants are shepherds, as our fathers were.' They said to Pharaoh, 'We have come to **sojourn** in the land, for there is no pasture for your servants' flocks, for the famine is severe in the land of Canaan. And now, please let your servants dwell in the land of Goshen.'"

In each of these cases, the patriarchs sojourned in order to escape the effects of famine. However, there is a major difference between when the patriarchs sojourned and when Elimelech sojourned. In the case of the patriarchs, the promise of the land had been given, but not the land itself. They were not yet settled in the land that Yahweh had promised them, and so by sojourning for a time they were not abandoning God's gifts. In fact, at least once, the command to sojourn came directly from God Himself. By the time Elimelech sojourned in Moab, the land had been given to the Israelites, and each tribe and clan had its own parcel of land. In light of this, the narrator prods the reader to ask: Is it possible that Elimelech was sinful for moving his family to Moab, a country that was pagan and an enemy of the Israelites? While the narrator himself does not pass judgment, other clues in the first five verses, as well as in other parts of Scripture, help us to answer this question.

Even as the reader begins to make connections between Elimelech and the patriarchs, the narrator hits the reader with a new wrinkle in verse 3: Elimelech's death. This death leaves Naomi widowed with her two sons in a foreign, pagan land. It is interesting that the verb *left* refers to Naomi specifically. The narrator does not say that Naomi and her two sons were left, but that Naomi was left with her two sons. This word order foreshadows Naomi's final condition of being the only one left and connects her with a major theme in the books of the prophets—the remnant. This theme will further develop as the Book of Ruth continues.

In verse 4, the narrator informs us that both of Naomi's sons "took Moabite wives." Note that to "take a wife" is a Hebrew idiom for marrying; it does not imply force or seizure of the woman. It is most often used in reference to marrying a foreign (non-Israelite) wife.[11] However, there should be other red flags going up about these marriages. Let's take a look at some key verses:

> **Deuteronomy 7:1–4:** "When the LORD your God brings you into the land that you are entering to take possession of it, and clears away many nations before you, the Hittites, the Girgashites, the Amorites, the Canaanites, the Perizzites, the Hivites, and the Jebusites, seven nations more numerous and mightier than you, and when the LORD your God gives them over to you, and you defeat them, then you must devote them to complete destruction. You shall make no covenant with them and show no mercy to them. You shall not intermarry with them, giving your daughters to their sons or taking their daughters for your sons, for they would turn away your sons from following Me, to serve other gods. Then the anger of the LORD would be kindled against you, and He would destroy you quickly."

> ◇   While marriage to Moabites is not specifically condemned here, the general idea of avoiding marriage to pagans and foreigners does apply. The reasoning is that intermarriage with nonbelievers will lead the Israelites astray such that they serve other gods.

> **Deuteronomy 23:3:** "No Ammonite or Moabite may enter the assembly of the LORD. Even to the tenth generation, none of them may enter the assembly of the LORD forever."

11   Wilch, 19.

◇   Given this direct command that Moabites may not enter the assembly of Yahweh, it should be clear that they are not suitable spouses. How can the family worship together if the Moabites may not enter the Lord's assembly?

Deuteronomy 21:10–14: "When you go out to war against your enemies, and the LORD your God gives them into your hand and you take them captive, and you see among the captives a beautiful woman, and you desire to take her to be your wife, and you bring her home to your house, she shall shave her head and pare her nails. And she shall take off the clothes in which she was captured and shall remain in your house and lament her father and her mother a full month. After that you may go in to her and be her husband, and she shall be your wife. But if you no longer delight in her, you shall let her go where she wants. But you shall not sell her for money, nor shall you treat her as a slave, since you have humiliated her."

> ◇ There is an exception to the rule. A man may marry a female captive during a war. Note that these rules are put in place not because they are the ideal way of things, but because the Lord is protecting them from their own sinfulness. If a man burns with lust, he can go about a proper way of marrying the woman. If, in his sinfulness, he is determined to then leave the captive, the Lord protects her from becoming a slave and lets her choose her own way in life. Furthermore, these verses are not prescriptive. That is, these are not "rules" or "regulations" or "guidelines" for how we should conduct ourselves today in a foreign war. These are descriptive of the specific commands Yahweh gave to the Israelites in anticipation of the conquest of the land. They apply to that time and place only. Of course, Mahlon and Chilion do not find themselves in this situation of wartime exception, yet they still marry foreign wives.

From these verses, it becomes clear that marriage to pagans was never a practice endorsed by God. Pagan spouses often led the faithful astray because they brought their own gods into the household. The guidelines in the Deuteronomy 21 passage requiring the woman to shave her head and put on sackcloth are a measure to try to create repentance. These actions should symbolize that she has turned away from not just her parents, but from her pagan gods as well. However, since Ruth and Orpah were not wives taken during war and therefore had not undergone the requirements of repentance as laid out in Deuteronomy 21, coupled with Orpah's easy return to Moab and Ruth's very expressive and sudden confession, it is clear that Mahlon and Chilion married unbelieving, pagan spouses.

Verse 5 puts major stress on the tragedy of the situation. The Hebrew wording includes three important constructions: (1) an intensifying adverb, (2) the plural of the word for "two," and (3) the inclusion of the names of the sons. (A more literal translation to English would be, "Then Mahlon and Chilion, indeed the two died.") Furthermore, the word translated as "sons" in this verse is the Hebrew word for young sons, in other words, "boys." This is not normally the term used for grown men who were sons. This word shows up in another significant verse, Ruth 4:16, which says: "Then Naomi took the child and laid him on her lap and became his nurse." The use of this word in both these places forms what is called an inclusio.[12] An inclusio is a word or phrase repeated at both ends of a narrative or a section of prose or poetry. This literary device has the effect of bracketing that entire section and connecting the beginning to the end to enhance the meaning of that section. By placing the same key word or phrase at the beginning and end, the narrator signals that the intervening verses or words are meant to be closely interpreted and inform one another. The key word or phrase unlocks the meaning of that section as a whole. There are several inclusios in Ruth. We'll see how well this particular inclusio connects when we get to chapter 4.

INTERPRETATION

Often in Hebrew narrative, it is left to the audience to take what they know about God's Law and the covenant and decide if the actions

---

12   Wilch 117.

of a character are right or wrong. In our case, the deaths of Elimelech, Mahlon, and Chilion stand out in the first part of this narrative. While the narrator does not explicitly say that their actions in leaving Israel and in taking pagan wives were wrong, it is important to note here that Elimelech's situation differed from that of the patriarchs who sojourned in that he had already received his plot of land while the patriarchs had only the promise of it.

According to law, each tribe was allocated a certain expanse of land. Out of that expanse, each clan was assigned its portion, and then the fields were divided by family group. But the land truly belonged to God; His gift of it to the Israelites was really a precursor of their eternal home with Him. The land was a tangible reminder of God's promises to provide for His people and to gather them to Himself. Therefore, the Israelites were to hold on to their plot of land and not let it pass out of the family.

The narrator may be implying that Elimelech's decision to leave his portion of the Promised Land during the famine could demonstrate a lack of faith. It is clear that Elimelech did not live up to his name: he did not see Yahweh as his King. At least, he did not see Yahweh as a King who comes to save, who will provide, and who is to be obeyed. Yahweh expressly forbids the selling of the land in Leviticus 25:23: "The land shall not be sold in perpetuity, for the land is Mine. For you are strangers and sojourners with Me." It may be the case, therefore, that Elimelech's death is a sign of Yahweh's judgment on him. The original hearers of Ruth would have known the laws and the commandments concerning the land (as we discussed on page 30). They would have recognized how Elimelech was being compared to the patriarchs. The narrator's language is specific enough to bring these ideas to mind and to point to this conclusion.

Additionally, think back to the passages we read from Deuteronomy concerning marriage. It is clear from these passages that marrying pagans was a slap in the face of God. Mahlon and Chilion's marriages in the Book of Ruth were not fruitful, which may have been an indication of Yahweh's judgment on them. Yahweh is the one who opens the womb and closes it. This truth that Yahweh controls the giving of life in the womb is constantly driven home in the lives of the matriarchs in Genesis. Sarah is barren, and Yahweh opens her womb. He does the same for Rachel and Leah. In the cases of the matriarchs, their barrenness is not related to any specific sin, but rather the truth that Yahweh opens their wombs points to His work in bringing about the Promised Seed. In Ruth, the implication that sin is what caused Yahweh to close their wombs is heavily hinted by the narrator. This idea of barrenness being a result of punishment in this instance in Ruth is not to be applied to the situation of every barren woman throughout time, however; Yahweh is doing and saying something specific in the life of Ruth. It is not a blanket statement that every barren woman has committed a specific sin that triggered her barrenness. Given the events recorded and the narrator's prompting, in the Book of Ruth we can draw a connection between barrenness and punishment, but we cannot do this in our own lives.[13] In the context of the Book of Ruth, and given Mahlon's and Chilion's unfruitful marriages to pagans, their deaths also suggest Yahweh's punishment.

When all is said and done, the narrator points to Naomi as the only one who is left (he does not refer to Ruth and Orpah as being left). This begs the questions: *Why is Naomi left? Why is she spared?* Ruth 1:8 helps to answer this question: "But Naomi said to her two daughters-in-law, 'Go, return each of you to her mother's house. May the LORD deal kindly with you, as you have dealt with the dead and with me.'" Naomi's use of God's name, Yahweh (which is what "LORD" in all capitals stands for), demonstrates that she still has faith in Yahweh. She has so much faith, in fact, that she speaks a blessing in His name on her pagan daughters-in-law. Her faithfulness is why she is left.

Someone being left is seen often throughout the Old Testament. For example, it is a common theme in the wilderness wanderings dur-

---

13   Those texts that show a correlation between barrenness and punishment are only descriptive of those particular instances. They are not prescriptive for all people of all time. This means that the correlation does not pertain to all people who have ever suffered through infertility. It cannot be asserted that barrenness is always a result of specific sin. In fact, it is only used in this way in very specific instances in the Scriptures, not in all. Hannah (1 Samuel) is an example of a woman who is barren with no indication that her barrenness has anything to do with a specific personal sin on her part. For more on this topic, see the section "Conception and Infertility" in Chapter 6, page 132.

ing the exodus. The Israelites wandered in the wilderness until the unfaithful generation died and only the faithful were left. When they worshiped the golden calf, three thousand were killed and only the faithful (those who did not worship the calf) were left (see Exodus 32).

There is also frequently a "remnant" theme in the prophets. Often, their prophecies show that Israel will be punished and reduced until only the faithful stump or remnant is left. As Isaiah puts it:

> There shall come forth a shoot from the stump of Jesse, and a branch from his roots shall bear fruit. . . . In that day the root of Jesse, who shall stand as a signal for the peoples—of Him shall the nations inquire, and His resting place shall be glorious. In that day the Lord will extend His hand yet a second time to recover the remnant that remains of His people, from Assyria, from Egypt, from Pathros, from Cush, from Elam, from Shinar, from Hamath, and from the coastlands of the sea. (Isaiah 11:1, 10–11)

Although seemingly cut off, the stump will bear fruit, and the remnant will be gathered to the Lord.

Naomi, then, is God's faithful remnant, and from the remnant will come His new faithful people. Furthermore, from the seed of that remnant will spring the seed of David and the seed promised in Genesis 3: the Messiah. But how will this be? We'll have to wait and find out how God will raise up His remnant.

Discussion Questions

1. Given the discussion of prophesy by way of typology or analogy, what are some other Old Testament scriptural events or persons that point forward to Christ and His gifts?

2. Recall the discussion about Elimelech and his relationship to the patriarchs. How was Elimelech's situation different than that of the patriarchs? How did Elimelech's actions demonstrate a lack of faith? What are some situations or life experiences that might present us with the same dilemma as Elimelech in prompting a lack of trust in God our Father?

3. Despite the ending Elimelech and his sons came to, how does Yahweh show grace and mercy to part of Elimelech's family? When we face difficult times and make mistakes, how does Yahweh show His grace and mercy to us?

CHAPTER 2

RUTH 1:6–22:
A STARTLING CONFESSION

OPENING PRAYER: O HOLY SPIRIT, Giver and
Strengthener of faith, grant that we, like Ruth, may confess
the one true God, Father, Son, and Holy Spirit, so others
may hear of Your great mercy and be brought to faith in
the waters of Holy Baptism, for You live and reign with the
Father and the Son, one God, now and forever. Amen.

Introduction

RIGHT AWAY IN THIS SECTION OF RUTH, the narrator offers the readers a literary technique—repetition—to help interpret the section. Biblical narrative relies heavily on repetition to show meaning and importance. One technique is *leitwort*. A German word, *leitwort* means "lead word." The *leitwort* of a section is a root word that is repeated throughout the section (see information on *leitwort* on page 15). In looking closely at the whole of verses 6–22, one verb should clearly stand out as the *leitwort*: turn/return.

Leitwort occurs when the semantic range of a root word is explored through repetition using synonymy (words meaning the same thing), antonymity (words that mean the opposite thing), and phonetic relatives (words that sound similar). *Leitwort* can indicate meaning and theme, and can also work within a motif (for example: righteous, righteousness, right, unrighteous). A common and well-known example of *leitwort* is found in Genesis 1. Repeatedly, God declares the creation to be "good." This teaches us that God's creation was good and pleasing to Him. On the final day, when He creates man, the *leitwort* changes just slightly. Any change or augmentation to the *leitwort* is usually important to understanding the overall idea being conveyed. On the final day of creation, God declares His creation to be "very good." This places man as the crowning glory of the creation and gives the reader the idea of completion and perfection.

In evaluating the use of *turn/return* in this section, it is important to note where the words are used in the narrative (such as in dialogue or at the beginning or end of the section). For instance, the verb is used immediately in verse 6, at the beginning of the section. Here the narrator is shifting our attention from the previous section of background information to the immediate action of the present time. The first action of Naomi and her daughters-in-law is to return from the fields of Moab to Israel/Judah. The verb also appears in many parts of the dialogue (vv. 8, 10, 11, 12, 15, and 16). Its repetition clearly shows that the act of returning or turning is a main focus of the section.

Turn/return appears in both verses 6 and 22. These two verses also have other vocabulary in common, such as "daughter-in-law" and "country of Moab." Given these close connections, it is safe to say that this section forms an *inclusio,* which we discussed in the previous chapter, and should be read closely as an important section in the overall narrative and as encapsulating a thematic message.

Given its prominence in this section, let's take a look at the verb *return.* In Hebrew, *return* can include the metaphorical meanings of "return to God" or "repent." Other important places in Scripture where someone "returns" include:

- Genesis 31:1–3: "Now Jacob heard that the sons of Laban were saying, 'Jacob has taken all that was our father's, and from what was our father's he has gained all this wealth.' And Jacob saw that Laban did not regard him with favor as before. Then the LORD said to Jacob, '**Return** to the land of your fathers and to your kindred, and I will be with you.'"
- Exodus 4:18–21: "Moses went back to Jethro his father-in-law and said to him, 'Please let me go back to my brothers in Egypt to see whether they are still alive.' And Jethro said to Moses, 'Go in peace.' And the LORD said to Moses in Midian, 'Go back to Egypt, for all the men who were seeking your life are dead.' So Moses took his wife and his sons and had them ride on a donkey, and went back to the land of Egypt. And Moses took the staff of God in his hand.

And the LORD said to Moses, 'When you go back to Egypt, see that you do before Pharaoh all the miracles that I have put in your power. But I will harden his heart, so that he will not let the people go.'" (ESV: "go back" is the same verb in Hebrew.)

- 1 Kings 19:15: "And the LORD said to him, 'Go, **return** on your way to the wilderness of Damascus. And when you arrive, you shall anoint Hazael to be king over Syria.'" (Elijah is called to return to Damascus after he fled the angry Jezebel.)

The preceding passages use the same Hebrew verb for *turn/return* that is used in the first section of Ruth. In each case, the people are told to return to their homelands, just as Naomi had decided to return to her homeland of Bethlehem.

The passages below use the metaphorical meaning of this verb to refer to turning back to God or repenting from sin:

- Psalm 80:3: "**Restore us**, O God; let Your face shine, that we may be saved!" ("Restore us" can also be translated as "turn us again" and is the same Hebrew verb as is used in Ruth.)

- Isaiah 10:20–21: "In that day the remnant of Israel and the survivors of the house of Jacob will no more lean on him who struck them, but will lean on the LORD, the Holy One of Israel, in truth. A remnant will **return**, the remnant of Jacob, to the mighty God." (Note the remnant theme. The "remnant" will return to God [from their sin].)

- Isaiah 59:20: "'And a Redeemer will come to Zion, to those in Jacob who **turn from** transgression,' declares the LORD."

- Jeremiah 3:12: "Go, and proclaim these words toward the north, and say, '**Return**, faithless Israel, declares the LORD. I will not look on you in anger, for I am merciful, declares the LORD; I will not be angry forever.'" (Israel is called to return to the Lord [from their unbelief/sin].)

Understanding all of the meanings of this *leitwort* is necessary to understanding the thematic aspects of this section as a whole, as well as some of the theological implications. As was said in the last chapter, Naomi is the only one left, which connects her to the remnant. Additionally, in the first five verses, the narrator purposely ties Elimelech and Naomi's story to the patriarchs and matriarchs. The use of the verb *turn/return* again strengthens the connection between Naomi and the remnant, who return, and the connection between Naomi and the patriarchs, who often also returned to their homelands after sojourning.

Keeping all of this in mind as background for this section, we can take a more in-depth look at each verse.

Verse-By-Verse Analysis
READ RUTH 1:6–22

In verse 6, a narrative shift takes place between setting the scene with background information and beginning the action of the story. The verb *arise* signals for us that the main action has begun. This verb is often used in Hebrew narration to show that the main action of the story is now taking place.[14] Interestingly, the verbs *arise* and *return* here are singular in the Hebrew. So although Naomi's daughters-in-law set out with her, the main focus in this verse and in the next (where the action verbs are also singular) is on Naomi. The narrator is focusing on her as the remnant who is returning to the Lord. Naomi's reason for returning to Moab is that she has heard that "[Yahweh] had visited His people and given them food" (v. 6); somehow she has learned of the end of the famine in the Promised Land.

Yahweh "visits" His people in two ways: in judgment and in mercy. Other instances when Yahweh "visited" His people include the wilderness wanderings and the exiles. In cases where God visits in judgment, this Hebrew verb is often rendered as "punish." Here are two examples:

- Isaiah 10:12: "When the Lord has finished all His work on Mount Zion and on Jerusalem, He will **punish** the speech of the arrogant heart of the king of Assyria and the boastful look in his eyes."
- Jeremiah 5:3, 6–9: "O LORD, do not Your eyes look for truth? You have struck them down, but they felt no anguish; You have consumed them, but they refused to take correction. They have

---
14   Wilch, 131.

made their faces harder than rock; they have refused to repent. . . . Therefore a lion from the forest shall strike them down; a wolf from the desert shall devastate them. A leopard is watching their cities; everyone who goes out of them shall be torn in pieces, because their transgressions are many, their apostasies are great. 'How can I pardon you? Your children have forsaken Me and have sworn by those who are no gods. When I fed them to the full, they committed adultery and trooped to the houses of whores. They were well-fed, lusty stallions, each neighing for his neighbor's wife. Shall I not **punish** them for these things? declares the LORD; and shall I not avenge Myself on a nation such as this?'" (verse 9 literally means "shall I not visit them . . . ?")

From these examples, it is clear that Yahweh does visit His people to punish them; however, note that He does so to bring about repentance, a repentance that gentle correction has not drawn forth from them (Jeremiah 5:3).

The time of the judges was a pretty dark time in Israel's history. Judges 21:25 states, "In those days there was no king in Israel. Everyone did what was right in his own eyes." "No king" does not mean just an earthly king; it also indicates that the Israelites did not view the Lord as their King. Remember that the opening verses of Ruth come on the heels of this statement of the unfaithfulness of God's people. We can conclude that God probably allowed the famine in Ruth as a sign of judgment. Note how chilling it is to read Judges 21:25 in conjunction with the first five verses of Ruth:

> In those days there was no king in Israel. Everyone did what was right in his own eyes.

> In the days when the judges ruled there was a famine in the land, and a man of Bethlehem in Judah went to sojourn in the country of Moab, he and his wife and his two sons. The name of the man was Elimelech and the name of his wife Naomi, and the names of his two sons were Mahlon and Chilion. They were Ephrathites from Bethlehem in Judah. They went into the country of Moab and remained there. But Elimelech, the husband of Naomi, died, and she was left with her two sons. These took Moabite wives; the name

of the one was Orpah and the name of the other Ruth. They lived there about ten years, and both Mahlon and Chilion died, so that the woman was left without her two sons and her husband. (Judges 21:25–Ruth 1:5)

Just as "everyone" did what was right in their own eyes and just as they did not regard God as their King, so Elimelech, in the face of famine, did what was right in his eyes and sojourned to the land of Moab, therefore failing to live up to his name, "my God is King." As we discussed in the previous chapter, Elimelech and his sons, like the whole of Israel so often did in the Book of Judges, experienced God's punishment. But the Lord's punishment is never His final word. The Lord visits in His wrath in order to evoke repentance and the return of His people. God's wrath is always in service to His mercy.

Yahweh, then, also visits His people in mercy. This mercy takes various forms, from "taking notice of" or "observing" their plight (same verb) to providing them with food. Ultimately, the Lord visits His people by sending His Son, Jesus, to save them from their sins and unrepentance. Here are some key passages regarding how Yahweh visits His people in mercy:

- Exodus 3:16: "Go and gather the elders of Israel together and say to them, 'The LORD, the God of your fathers, the God of Abraham, of Isaac, and of Jacob, has appeared to me, saying, "**I have observed you** and what has been done to you in Egypt."'"
- Exodus 4:31: "And the people believed; and when they heard that the LORD had **visited** the people of Israel and that He had seen their affliction, they bowed their heads and worshiped."

In these two verses from Exodus, the Lord visits His people to free them from slavery to the Egyptians. In 3:16, the verb is translated as "I have observed you." This points to the idea that the Lord has visited His people and has not only seen them but will act on their affliction. In 4:31, Moses, through Aaron, relays this message to the people in words and signs, and they recognize the Lord's merciful visitation.

That the Lord also visits His people in order to provide for daily needs is clear from Psalm 132:15, where the Lord states, "I will abundantly bless her provisions; I will satisfy her poor with bread." We pray for such daily visitation in the Lord's Prayer when we petition the Lord to "give us this day our daily bread."

Finally, God visits His people and the whole world in mercy as is demonstrated by Luke 1:68–69: "Blessed be the Lord God of Israel, for He has **visited** and redeemed His people and has raised up a horn of salvation for us in the house of His servant David." The horn of salvation is raised up through David and is, of course, Jesus. God's final word and final mode of visitation is always merciful in Christ Jesus.

Based, then, on our discussions of the *leitwort* of this section, as well as Naomi's recognition of the Lord's merciful visitation of His people, Naomi's return to Judah implies not only a physical turning, but a spiritual one as well. She is returning to Yahweh and still clings to Him by faith.

Naomi's faith is shown even more clearly in her first burst of dialogue, verses 8 and 9. In Hebrew narrative, the first words a person speaks are extremely important to understanding his or her character; they tell us about the personality or faith of the person. Naomi's first words are in a prayer or blessing format. We will encounter several prayers or blessings throughout Ruth that point to a character's faith that Yahweh will answer his or her prayer. The narrator leaves us here with a question: How will Naomi's prayer be answered?

To begin with, Naomi commands her daughters-in-law to return to their families. By returning to their parental homes, they have more opportunity to remarry and have a good life, as their parents can arrange for new husbands for them. As long as Naomi stays in Moab, her daughters-in-law are obligated to her. Because Naomi is a foreigner, it would be nearly impossible for her to find husbands for them. Naomi sacrifices for their sakes both by urging them to leave her and in her willingness to make the rest of the journey by herself.[15] (Note that in this verse, *return* is used differently to describe the return to Moab of the daughters-in-law.)

---

15   For more on this idea, see Wilch, 155.

Naomi asks a blessing for her daughters-in-law from Yahweh. In the blessing, the word translated as "deal kindly" (ESV) or "show kindness" (NIV)—*chesed*—is a very important word in the Old Testament. *Chesed* is better understood as faithfulness, especially within the context of Ruth. It is also often translated as "steadfast love." It denotes the Lord's faithfulness to His people because of His covenant promise to them, even when they are unfaithful. Naomi is asking God to bless them in the manner in which He blesses His covenant people. It is a bold and living prayer on Naomi's part.

Other instances of the use of the word *chesed* can help us to better understand its full meaning:

- Genesis 39:21: "But the LORD was with Joseph and showed him **steadfast love** and gave him favor in the sight of the keeper of the prison."
- Exodus 15:13: "You have led in Your **steadfast love** the people whom You have redeemed; You have guided them by Your strength to Your holy abode." (This is from the song of Moses and the Israelites after crossing the Red Sea.)
- Exodus 20:5–6: "You shall not bow down to them or serve them, for I the LORD your God am a jealous God, visiting the iniquity of the fathers on the children to the third and the fourth generation of those who hate Me, but showing **steadfast love** to thousands of those who love Me and keep My commandments."
- Exodus 34:6–7: "The LORD passed before him and proclaimed, 'The LORD, the LORD, a God merciful and gracious, slow to anger, and abounding in **steadfast love and faithfulness**, keeping **steadfast love** for thousands, forgiving iniquity and transgression and sin, but who will by no means clear the guilty, visiting the iniquity of the fathers on the children and the children's children, to the third and the fourth generation.'"
- God has shown "steadfast love" to a very important person in the Old Testament: David. 1 Kings 3:6: "And Solomon said, 'You have shown great and **steadfast love** to Your servant David my father, because he walked before You in faithfulness, in righteous-

ness, and in uprightness of heart toward You. And You have kept for him this great and **steadfast love** and have given him a son to sit on his throne this day.'"

By asking Yahweh to show *chesed* to her daughters-in-law, Naomi is asking Him to act in His covenantal mercy and promises toward even these pagan women. She is holding Yahweh to who He is and promises to be for His people: a God of steadfast love, faithfulness, and mercy.

Naomi's covenant wishes for her daughters-in-law continue in verse 9, where she expresses hope that they "find rest." This can also be understood as "security." (*Rest* [or *security*] is a part of God's covenant blessings to His people.) By expressing this hope, Naomi displays her faithfulness to and familiarity with Yahweh's Word.

Rest can refer to a place or a time of rest:

- Exodus 20:8–11: "Remember the Sabbath day, to keep it holy. Six days you shall labor, and do all your work, but the seventh day is a Sabbath to the LORD your God. On it you shall not do any work, you, or your son, or your daughter, your male servant, or your female servant, or your livestock, or the sojourner who is within your gates. For in six days the LORD made heaven and earth, the sea, and all that is in them, and **rested** on the seventh day. Therefore the LORD blessed the Sabbath day and made it holy."

- Deuteronomy 12:8–11: "You shall not do according to all that we are doing here today, everyone doing whatever is right in his own eyes, for you have not as yet come to the **rest** and to the inheritance that the LORD your God is giving you. But when you go over the Jordan and live in the land that the LORD your God is giving you to inherit, and when He gives you **rest** from all your enemies around, so that you live in safety, then to the place that the LORD your God will choose, to make His name dwell there, there you shall bring all that I command you: your burnt offerings and your sacrifices, your tithes and the contribution that you present, and all your finest vow offerings that you vow to the LORD." (The Israelites will find their place of rest in the land God will give to them, and they will then be able to better observe the Sabbath day of rest, as well.)

- Joshua 1:12–13: "And to the Reubenites, the Gadites, and the half-tribe of Manasseh Joshua said, 'Remember the word that Moses the servant of the LORD commanded you, saying, "The LORD your God is providing you a **place of rest** and will give you this land."'" (The land is again referred to as a place of rest.)
- Isaiah 32:18: "My people will abide in a peaceful habitation, in secure dwellings, and in quiet **resting places**."

The *rest* referred to in Yahweh's covenant blessings can also refer to one that comes only from God and has to do with His presence and His resting place, and one that goes beyond this earthly life:

- Exodus 33:14: "And He said, 'My presence will go with you, and I will give you **rest**.'" (This verse refers to the fact that the Lord's presence would go with the Israelites on their journeys. The rest promised is directly related to God's presence in their midst.)
- Psalm 132:8, 13–14: "Arise, O LORD, and go to Your **resting place**, You and the ark of Your might. . . . For the LORD has chosen Zion; He has desired it for His dwelling place: 'This is My **resting place** forever; here I will dwell, for I have desired it.'" (When the Lord is in His resting place [the sanctuary], then His people also have rest.)

All forms of rest are gifts of Yahweh to His covenant people, not because of their faithfulness but because of His faithfulness and His presence dwelling with them. Naomi's prayer for her daughters-in-law asks for all of these aspects of rest. It is a bold request, yet Naomi trusts in the Lord's mercy and faithfulness and expects the Lord to answer her prayer.

> **"And they lifted up their voices and wept"** (Ruth 1:9): After Naomi offers the blessing, the daughters-in-law begin to mourn for her leaving. Weeping loudly is a typical Middle Eastern expression of genuine grief and sorrow and gives import to the loss being experienced. By the time of the New Testament, professional mourners could be hired to augment the grieving process for an important person. The more mourners and the louder the display, the more important the person must have been. Several times when Jesus intends to raise someone from the dead, He drives the wailing mourners out of the house (see, for example Mark 5:35–42). In the end, the Lord Himself will end all need for mourning and weeping.

In verses 10 through 14, the daughters-in-law respond to Naomi's urging using the *leitwort* of this section when they protest, "No, we will return with you to your people" (v. 10). Here they align themselves with Naomi's situation and perspective. She is returning, so they are taking on her terms, and they are also returning, although they have never been to Judah. Naomi's reply uses three rhetorical questions or scenarios to dissuade her daughters-in-law. The questions become less plausible as they progress. First, she reminds them of her age by asking, "Have I yet sons in my womb?" The answer is no; it should be obvious that as an older, widowed woman, Naomi has no sons in her womb. Next, she notes that she is too old even to have a husband, but she offers another nearly impossible scenario with the possibility of a husband and conceiving that very night. By verse 13, Naomi reaches the height of her nonsense argument. She refers to Orpah and Ruth, waiting for other sons to be born and grow up so they can be husbands to them. Even if the other scenarios were to come to pass, how could the younger women wait so many years for the sons to be grown? Naomi's argument references the practice of Levirate marriage, wherein a brother of a man who died childless would marry his widow and provide an heir in order to continue the deceased's inheritance and his name. This practice comes up again later in Ruth, so we will explore it more then.

In verses 11–13, Naomi implies that all of this is impossible, but it is not her age, her reproductive status, or even the lack of a husband, really, which makes it so. What makes it impossible, she says, is that "the hand of the LORD has gone out against" her; therefore a Levirate marriage or other provision is impossible for Orpah and Ruth if they stay with her. The subtext is that the Lord would overcome all of these issues if He wanted to do so. After all, Sarah conceived in her old age, He gave Tamar conception while she was waiting to be given another of Judah's sons, and He will give conception to the Virgin Mary. Of course, Mary could not have been on Naomi's mind as she presented these scenarios, but she may very well have been thinking of Sarah and Tamar. She knows that Yahweh could overcome her seemingly impossible situation, but as His hand has gone out against her, this, she believes, will not happen. The idea of the "hand of the LORD" is similar to that of the Lord "visiting" His people. Yahweh's hand goes out either in wrath or in grace and mercy. Naomi believes that Yahweh's hand has gone against her in wrath, and her circumstances certainly point her to this belief. It is interesting that while she trusts Yahweh to show grace and mercy to her pagan daughters-in-law, as shown by her prayer for them, she does not expect this same mercy for herself. She feels herself to be under God's Law.

It sounds a lot like Naomi is complaining. She is certainly holding Yahweh accountable for her misfortune. Is this a little sinful? Our gut reaction is to think that it is. We shouldn't complain to God, right? This situation is not His doing, is it?

It might be helpful to explore some other verses and ask ourselves who else in the Bible complains to the Lord.

- Job 19:21: "Have mercy on me, have mercy on me, O you my friends, for the hand of God has touched me!"
- Jeremiah 8:19, 22: "Behold, the cry of the daughter of my people from the length and breadth of the land: 'Is the LORD not in Zion? Is her King not in her?' 'Why have they provoked Me to anger with their carved images and with their foreign idols?' . . . Is there no balm in Gilead? Is there no physician there? Why then has the health of the daughter of my people not been restored?"
- Jeremiah 12:1–4: "Righteous are You, O LORD, when I complain to You; yet I would plead my case before You. Why does the way

of the wicked prosper? Why do all who are treacherous thrive? You plant them, and they take root; they grow and produce fruit; You are near in their mouth and far from their heart. But You, O LORD, know me; You see me, and test my heart toward You. Pull them out like sheep for the slaughter, and set them apart for the day of slaughter. How long will the land mourn and the grass of every field wither? For the evil of those who dwell in it the beasts and the birds are swept away, because they said, 'He will not see our latter end.'"

In Ruth 1:13, Naomi acknowledges that Yahweh is the author of all of life and that nothing happens in this life without His hand. This demonstrates her faith that Yahweh is in control of her life. However, "Yahweh is in control" is not always a comforting thought. Job also teaches us that Yahweh is in control, and in his case especially, this is both a harrowing and a comforting thought. If God is in control, then He controls the devil's tormenting of Job short of taking his life (the caveat God states in Job 2:1–6). So Job is right to note that it *is* Yahweh's hand that has "touched" him and caused his affliction. Similarly, Jeremiah expresses his anguish, and the thoughts of all the people, when the Lord seems to be absent from Zion: Where is our King? Is there no balm in Gilead?

Even as he asks these questions, Jeremiah looks to Yahweh as the one who acts and the one who can reverse the situation. Jeremiah boldly pleads his case before Yahweh, even as he acknowledges that he is complaining. He believes that Yahweh will answer his pleading. Job, too, clings not to the Yahweh who is "in control" so demonstrably of his afflictions, but to the Redeemer who will plead his case before Yahweh and to Yahweh's merciful nature (see especially Job 19).

Yahweh can handle our complaints, especially when we take them to Him in prayer and pleading. Although Naomi may differ from Job and Jeremiah in that she does not seem to trust that God's grace is for *her*, she trusts that it can still be there for others.

In verse 14, Orpah and Ruth respond to Naomi by again weeping loudly. Then their actions differ from each other. Orpah's kiss is a farewell; she will return to her home. But Ruth clings to Naomi. This word is an interesting choice for this moment, because it can be used to describe the relationship between husband and wife. The word *cling* first appears in Scripture in the account of the marriage of Adam and Eve. Genesis 2:24 reads: "Therefore a man shall leave his father and his mother and **hold fast** to his wife, and they shall become one flesh." (the same word is used in both Genesis 2:24 and Ruth 1:14.) Clinging or holding fast is a strong description of a close relationship. To cling is to hold tightly, not to give a side-arm hug or a handshake.

The term can also refer to Israel's ideal covenant relationship with Yahweh. As we know, one metaphor for Yahweh and His people is often that of a bride and groom. Yahweh is the groom and His people (first Israel and then the new Israel, the Church) are His Bride. Yahweh clings to His people through His promises, and His people cling to Him in faith. Joshua 22:5 puts it this way: "Only be very careful to observe the commandment and the law that Moses the servant of the LORD commanded you, to love the LORD your God, and to walk in all His ways and to keep His commandments and to cling to Him and to serve Him with all your heart and with all your soul." Here Joshua reminds the people to cling to Yahweh above all. Ruth clings to Naomi with the same fierceness and commitment as in a marriage relationship and as in the covenant relationship between Yahweh and His people. Her actions are startling, but in a moment her words will be even more so.

This section finds its peak in verses 15–18, where Ruth makes her startling confession. As Orpah has turned and left, Naomi notes that she is going back to "her people and her gods." We conclude from these words that Orpah is still a pagan; she could be returning to her local gods and relinquishing the faith of Naomi. Naomi urges Ruth to do likewise, but Ruth has something else to say on the matter. Ruth very directly refutes Naomi's urging to return. This is set up in a *chiasm,* a literary convention whereby the main thrust of a section is set in the center of related matching parts of the section. The pattern is usually ABCB'A'. It can also often be diagrammed as an X with the center portion at the apex of the X. Ruth's speech can be diagrammed in this way:

A Plea against force: "Do not urge me to leave you or to return from following you."

> *B Promise of accompaniment in life: "For where you go I will go, and where you lodge I will lodge."*

> C Promise of ethnic and religious identity: "Your people shall be my people, and your God my God."

> *B' Promise of accompaniment in death: "Where you die I will die, and there will I be buried."*

A' Oath against separation: "May the Lord do so to me and more also if anything but death parts me from you."[16]

As can be seen from this diagram, Ruth's speech has corresponding parts. The first and last lines are similar types of speech (a plea and an oath). The second and fourth lines are promises of accompaniment and have to do with life and death. This leaves the central portion of Ruth's speech as a confession: "Your people will be my people and your God will be my God." In other words, she identifies fully with Naomi and the Israelite people, and she professes that Yahweh is her God. Ruth is leaving behind her pagan gods, her identity, and her family. Unlike Orpah, she will not return to "her people and her gods," as Naomi has asked.

Again, in Hebrew narrative, the first dialogue of any character is important to note and often reveals the personality or another important aspect of that character. Ruth's speech reveals that she is decisive—she gets to the point quickly and poetically. It also reveals her faith in Yahweh; the first thing we hear from Ruth is a strong vow based on a profession of faith in Yahweh.

---

16   This diagram of the chiasm is taken from Wilch, 169.

Additionally, a literary device called merism, very common in Hebrew writing, is employed here in Ruth's speech. Merism, by stating two opposites or extremes, covers everything in between. Ruth's speech uses merism when she promises to accompany Naomi in life and in death. By mentioning both of these aspects of the human experience, Ruth is telling Naomi that her commitment to her is all-encompassing and never-ending.

The final surprise and most striking aspect of Ruth's speech is that she uses the covenant name of God, showing that she is a true believer. Only the covenant people of God were given the gift of knowing and properly using His personal name, Yahweh. This is the name revealed to Moses in Exodus 3 and used by the patriarchs and matriarchs. Wilch also notes that this verse is often mistranslated and should be translated as a conditional sentence: "Thus may Yahweh do to me, and do even more so, if death will separate me and you!"[17] In other words, Ruth is saying that her vow to Naomi is so strong that not even death will separate them. This seems to convey that Ruth believes in the resurrection. The belief in life after death and in a resurrection is not uncommon in the Old Testament (see 1 Samuel 28:14–20 and Job 19 for examples). Ruth's clinging to Naomi will last not just for their present earthly life, but into life eternal as well. So strong is this vow that Naomi, for the first time in this section, is reduced to silence. She has no more clever rhetorical questions, no more prayers or blessings, and no more statements urging Ruth's departure.

After this section of dialogue, the narrator breaks back in to advance the action to their arrival in Bethlehem (Ruth 1:19–22). Once they have arrived at their destination, Naomi and Ruth encounter the women, who ask, "Is this Naomi?" These women are incredulous, perhaps even unsure if she is really who she says she is. Naomi urges the women not to call her by her given name, but rather to call her "Mara." *Mara* means "bitter." She referred to herself this way in the previous section when she urged her daughters-in-law to return to Moab (1:12–13). Remember that Naomi's name means "pleasant." Now she

---

17   Wilch, 130.

is saying that her life, and perhaps her personality, no longer reflects pleasantness but instead reflects bitterness. Interestingly enough, this verb for "bitter" also occurs in Exodus 15:22–25a:

> Then Moses made Israel set out from the Red Sea, and they went into the wilderness of Shur. They went three days in the wilderness and found no water. When they came to Marah, they could not drink the water of Marah because it was bitter; therefore it was named Marah. And the people grumbled against Moses, saying, "What shall we drink?" And he cried to the LORD, and the LORD showed him a log, and he threw it into the water, and the water became sweet.

Here the Lord takes what is bitter and makes it sweet for the sake of and at the prayers of His people. The question is: Will He do the same for Naomi?

Naomi expands on her request for a name change by explaining that Yahweh has dealt bitterly with her and brought her home empty. He has testified against her and brought calamity upon her. The word for empty here refers both to possessions (such as food) and to family. Naomi is bereft of both. Naomi does not mention Ruth; she seems to ignore Ruth's presence or is not able to acknowledge Ruth or see her as connected to her complaints. This suggests that Naomi is unable to see the help that Yahweh has given her. She is stuck in her grief and inwardly focused. So while it is not necessarily wrong for her to be angry with God or to complain against Him, Naomi still has a problem. She has allowed her bitterness to consume her and turn her focus upon herself. She is wrapped up in herself and cannot see the solutions God may already be forming for her.

Again, the narrator breaks into the story. (Anytime the narrator breaks into the action of the story, we should sit up and pay attention.) The narrator reminds us of what Naomi seems to have forgotten: Ruth had returned with her. Notice how much emphasis the narrator places on this by naming her in three different ways: "Ruth," "the Moabite," and "her daughter-in-law." In this, the narrator points the reader to the responses God has already offered to Naomi's complaints. The narrator indicates that Ruth is an answer to Naomi's bitterness and emptiness. Naomi is no longer "left" alone as the only remnant, because

Ruth remains with her. Furthermore, the narrator shows the reader how God is poised to provide. Ruth and Naomi have arrived in Bethlehem (which means "House of Bread") at the time of the barley harvest. Through Ruth, and through the harvest, God is working to fill at least one aspect of Naomi's emptiness, even if she cannot yet see it.

INTERPRETATION

Like Naomi, we have all encountered times of struggle, emptiness, bitterness, and pain. Like Job and Jeremiah, we have felt the hand of the Lord come out against us for sometimes seemingly inexplicable reasons. We have felt as though He is absent and not working in our lives. We have not been able to see His work behind the scenes. We have asked, "Where is the Lord?" and "Is there no balm in Gilead?" Often, God in His hiddenness seems distant, cruel, and arbitrary. The temptation in those times is to try to figure out what God is doing and why. Have we sinned in some specific way? Is God trying to tell us something about how we need to change or do something differently? Or perhaps, like Naomi, we resign ourselves to our suffering and turn ever inward, wallowing in our misery and blocking out all around us.

It is not to God's hiddenness that we should look in times of struggle and pain. It is not to ourselves that we should turn. Rather, we look to God in His revealed self. God reveals Himself in mercy in Jesus Christ and Him crucified. It is to Him we cling, like Ruth clung to Naomi and like God clings to us. Clinging to Christ crucified, we ride out the storm brought on by God in His hiddenness (see Isaiah 45:7 and chapter 3, page 41). We take solace in the Church, where God's revealed Means of Grace are found, remembering our Baptisms and partaking of the Lord's Supper. And sometimes, when we come out on the other end, we can look back and see the marks of God's other means for working mercy—the people who love us, the random strangers encountered on the way, the timing of everything—although we could not see these things before. For Naomi, God hid Himself in Ruth and in the timing of their return. What He works through those two things is amazing.

Questions for Discussion:

1. Can we approach God with our laments? What are some examples from Scripture that show us how to plead with God in difficult times?

2. How does the phrase "God is in control" cut both ways with regard to terror and comfort?

3. How does the narrator help us to peek into God's hidden work behind the scenes in the Book of Ruth?

4. Can you think of a time in your life when things looked dark and God seemed distant? To what did you cling during that time? How did God in Christ eventually reveal His gracious self? How might we bring comfort to others in such times? Where should they look?

5. What did we say was the peak point of this section and why?

6. Discuss the return/turn theme of this section. How is that developed throughout the section and what are its theological implications?

7. What are some of the ways in both this section and the previous one that the narrator connects Naomi to the matriarchs and patriarchs (i.e., Abraham, Isaac, Rebekah, Leah, Sarah, Rachel, Jacob, etc.) and to the remnant theme?

CHAPTER 3

RUTH 2: GLEANINGS

OPENING PRAYER: HEAVENLY FATHER, You provide for all of our daily needs of body and soul; help us to trust, like Ruth, in Your care and providence so that we may testify to others of Your faithfulness, for You live and reign with the Son and the Holy Spirit, one God, now and forever. Amen.

Introduction to Ruth Chapter 2

AS WE NOTED AT THE END OF THE first chapter of Ruth, Yahweh seems to have abandoned Naomi and left her without family, food, or income—yet He is poised to uniquely fill her emptiness through some very ordinary means. The narrator, by taking a break from the action of the story to summarize things at the end of chapter 1, reminds the reader that Yahweh has two means by which He will begin to fill Naomi's emptiness: the first is Ruth, and the second is the barley harvest. In God's hands, such ordinary things as a person and the timing of Naomi's return have extraordinary results. This is how our Lord prefers to act, after all. He likes to use ordinary means to bring about His saving work: means such as water, bread, and wine. When these ordinary things are combined with God's Word and His promise, they bring about His salvation and deliver it to us. In a similar way, Yahweh will use Ruth and the barley harvest to begin His gracious work in Naomi's life.

Verse by Verse Analysis
READ RUTH 2:1–23

In these verses, the narrator once again pauses before continuing the action of the story. By introducing Boaz in the first verse, the narrator is foreshadowing things to come in this chapter. But the verse itself, apart from understanding it as the narrator's little hint to the reader, seems strangely placed. In the midst of discussing the arrival of Ruth and Naomi, the narrator abruptly inserts a sentence about someone named Boaz and then dives back into the narrative action in verse 2. This hint is to show how Yahweh is already working to bring about help for Naomi.

Boaz is related to Naomi by marriage; he is a relative of Elimelech. This tidbit is important because it shows the reader that there is a possibility for something similar to Levirate marriage and the restoration of Elimelech's line. Furthermore, Boaz is not just any relative; he is a "worthy man" or a man "of standing." The Hebrew word used here can mean a variety of things: strong, mighty, valiant, or wealthy. It can also mean having honor or being honorable. This word appears again in chapter 3, and its consistent translation shows the connections between the chapters. Boaz may be wealthy or have some wealth, but it becomes clear from context that this word has more to do with who he is as a person than with his bank account.

In verse 2, the narrator shifts back to the main action of the story. This is made evident by the inclusion of dialogue. Dialogue is not used just for the sake of making the story more interesting. Rather, dialogue is the main conveyance of important information in biblical narrative. It also ties in with the foreshadowing done by the narrator. The narrator has mentioned a "worthy man," and Ruth asks to go and glean in the fields after "him in whose sight I shall find favor." As readers, we may safely assume that Ruth will meet with Boaz in this chapter. Also notice that it is Ruth who does most of the speaking in this verse. Aside from Naomi's permissive response, Ruth is the one who takes initiative and has a plan to help them survive. In the Hebrew, there is a word here that means "please," but it often is not translated. It should be, because it shows Ruth's submissiveness to Naomi. While Ruth takes the initiative, she defers to Naomi by saying, "Please let me go."

Ruth is asking to "glean" in the fields, to follow behind the reapers and pick up the grains left lying on the ground. This is not a strange request; gleaning was common at the time. In fact, Leviticus 19:9–10 and 23:22 reveal that God commanded the Israelites to leave the edges of the fields unharvested and leave the gleanings in the field for the sojourners and the poor. And in Deuteronomy 24:19–21, He commands the Israelites to leave sheaves for the sojourner, the fatherless, and the poor.

Commands Regarding the Harvest and the Poor

Leviticus 19:9–10: "When you reap the harvest of your land, you shall not reap your field right up to its edge, neither shall you gather the gleanings after your harvest. And you shall not strip your vineyard bare, neither shall you gather the fallen grapes of your vineyard. You shall leave them for the poor and for the sojourner: I am the LORD your God."

Leviticus 23:22: "And when you reap the harvest of your land, you shall not reap your field right up to its edge, nor shall you gather the gleanings after your harvest. You shall leave them for the poor and for the sojourner: I am the LORD your God."

Deuteronomy 24:19–21: "When you reap your harvest in your field and forget a sheaf in the field, you shall not go back to get it. It shall be for the sojourner, the fatherless, and the widow, that the LORD your God may bless you in all the work of your hands. When you beat your olive trees, you shall not go over them again. It shall be for the sojourner, the fatherless, and the widow. When you gather the grapes of your vineyard, you shall not strip it afterward. It shall be for the sojourner, the fatherless, and the widow."

These commandments from God are not separate or random. They grow out of the Ten Commandments. Such provision in the fields is one of the ways to love your neighbor as yourself, the summary of the second table of the Commandments. Luther's explanation of the Fifth Commandment in the Small Catechism includes both the negative and the positive meanings of the commandment not to murder: "We should fear and love God so that we do not hurt or harm our neighbor in his body, but *help and support him in every physical need.*"[18] The commandment to leave sheaves in the field and edges unharvested is an example of how to understand the positive aspect of the Fifth Commandment; it is one way to help and support your neighbor in his or

18 Martin Luther, *Luther's Small Catechism with Explanation*, (St. Louis: Concordia Publishing House, 1986, 1991, reprint 2005), 12. My emphasis.

her physical needs. This demonstrates the spirit of the Law and goes beyond the letter of it. Not only should you not harm your neighbor directly, but you should also attend to your neighbor in need.

Even with this commandment protecting the right of the sojourner, widow, and fatherless to glean, Ruth is still concerned with finding someone who will look on her with favor. This seems strange, but it is an indication of the sad fact that sometimes such careful attention to the *spirit* of the Ten Commandments was lacking among the Israelites (and indeed among all people, including us). See the following verses:

- Isaiah 1:23: "Your princes are rebels and companions of thieves. Everyone loves a bribe and runs after gifts. They do not bring justice to the fatherless, and the widow's cause does not come to them."
- Isaiah 10:1–2: "Woe to those who decree iniquitous decrees, and the writers who keep writing oppression, to turn aside the needy from justice and to rob the poor of My people of their right, that widows may be their spoil, and that they may make the fatherless their prey!"
- Psalm 94:6: "They kill the widow and the sojourner, and murder the fatherless."

Although Yahweh has tried to teach compassion and the spirit of the Law to His people, sinfulness rears its ugly head, and those who are most in need of help and love are ignored or even accosted. Therefore, Ruth is putting herself at risk by going to glean in the fields. This is why she is concerned with seeking someone with whom she will "find favor." So not only is Ruth the one to take the initiative in providing for them, but she is also willing to take a great personal risk to do so. This shows us that Ruth, though formerly a pagan, is able to see and understand the spirit of the Law. Unlike the Israelites in the verses above, who should recognize and act according to the Law gifted to them, Ruth is the one who goes above and beyond its letter in order to serve Naomi.

In verse 3, then, Ruth "happened to come" to Boaz's plot of land. (Recall that just two verses prior, the narrator assured the reader that

Boaz was a worthy man and a kinsman of Naomi's.) The phrase "and she happened to come" is actually more accurately translated, "and she happened upon her happenstance." This redundancy indicates something more than fate or good luck. Naomi has already testified that Yahweh is in control of *everything*, and other verses support this point:

- Lamentations 3:37–38: "Who has spoken and it came to pass, unless the Lord has commanded it? Is it not from the mouth of the Most High that good and bad come?"

- Isaiah 45:1–8: "Thus says the LORD to His anointed, to Cyrus, whose right hand I have grasped, to subdue nations before him and to loose the belts of kings, to open doors before him that gates may not be closed: 'I will go before you and level the exalted places, I will break in pieces the doors of bronze and cut through the bars of iron, I will give you the treasures of darkness and the hoards in secret places, that you may know that it is I, the LORD, the God of Israel, who call you by your name. For the sake of My servant Jacob, and Israel My chosen, I call you by your name, I name you, though you do not know Me. I am the LORD, and there is no other, besides Me there is no God; I equip you, though you do not know Me, that people may know, from the rising of the sun and from the west, that there is none besides Me; I am the LORD, and there is no other. I form light and create darkness, I make well-being and create calamity, I am the LORD, who does all these things. 'Shower, O heavens, from above, and let the clouds rain down righteousness; let the earth open, that salvation and righteousness may bear fruit; let the earth cause them both to sprout; I the LORD have created it.'"

The narrator then, is making it clear to us that Ruth's "happening to happen" upon Boaz's field is no accident. With a wink and a nod, the narrator points us to Yahweh's hand without saying His name specifically. Yahweh has made sure that Ruth would find this field. And by this, He is answering Naomi's prayers and laments concerning her emptiness. He has prepared a way for Ruth to safely glean, which begins to fulfill their physical emptiness.

In verses 4 through 7, we are introduced to Boaz, who immediately takes an interest in Ruth. The narrator presents Boaz as a surprise to Ruth, using the term *behold*, which was the Hebrew way of saying "Surprise! Pay attention!" Not only does Ruth happen upon Boaz's field, but she happens upon it on a day when Boaz himself had come to supervise the harvest. The greetings between Boaz and his reapers are pretty standard, but they do tell us something about what kind of man he is. Boaz greets his workers in the name of the Lord, indicating his faith in Him. After greeting his workers, Boaz's first order of business is to understand who Ruth is. He calls her a "young woman," giving us a clue to her age. Boaz's foreman gives an account of Ruth's ethnicity, her relationship to Naomi, and why she is in the fields. She asked to "please" be allowed to glean behind the reapers. The Hebrew in the last part of verse 7 is translated different ways. It may mean that she took only a short rest, that that rest was in a shelter, or that she was resting at that very moment. However, this detail does not have an impact on the story, so differing translations are not a cause for concern. The bottom line is that Ruth had worked hard so far during the day with little or no rest.

The foreman repeats Ruth's request to glean "behind the reapers." In Israel, this was the process for the harvest:

1. The reapers would grasp a handful of stalks with one hand.

2. With the other hand, they would cut it using a sickle.

3. They would lay the handful of cut grain on the ground behind them.

4. These handfuls were then gathered and bundled by the "bundler."

5. The bundles were then bound into sheaves and gathered. They would be removed from the fields completely.

6. Gleaners could glean only in the parts of the field where the sheaves had already been removed to the threshing floor. [19]

---

19   The historical information concerning the harvest is summarized from: Frederic W. Bush, *Ruth, Esther:* Word Biblical Commentary, (Dallas: Word Books, 1996), 114.

Ruth asked to glean "behind the reapers," as in, at the end of their work, probably after the sheaves had been removed to the threshing floor.

Upon hearing this account, Boaz directly addresses Ruth. He tells her to stay close to his young women, who were probably the bundlers who gathered everything into sheaves and removed them. The verb used to tell Ruth to remain with his young women, translated as "keep close" (ESV) or "stay here" (NIV), is the same verb used in Ruth 1:14: cling (Hebrew: *dabaq*). Boaz tells her that she can follow *very* closely after the young women. Permission to follow so closely gives her protection and the opportunity to glean more grain. This was an unusual command for a worthy man to give to a mere gleaner.

Boaz goes a step further to protect and provide for Ruth by giving a command to the young men who work for him. In verse 9, the statement might be better translated, "Do I not hereby command . . .?" The command is accomplished the moment it is spoken.[20] In other words, Boaz is addressing both his workers and Ruth as he commands them to treat her well and assures her that his word will be obeyed.

In that same verse, Boaz grants a further privilege to Ruth by allowing her to drink water from the vessels reserved for his workers. These are privileges and rights that are not necessarily granted to the widow, sojourner, and poor for whom gleaning was permitted. Boaz, like Ruth, begins to go above and beyond the letter of the Law. Ruth acknowledges his kindness by prostrating herself before him. This was a typical way of bowing at the time, in which the person bowed very low to the ground or laid face down on it. Such a gesture was a sign of respect and gratitude.

Ruth's subsequent question has two parts: she wonders why she has "found favor" and why Boaz has "taken notice" of her. Notice, first, that her use of "found favor" echoes her own earlier statement that she wanted to go into the fields and glean behind someone with whom she would find favor. This sort of mini-prayer is answered by Boaz's kindnesses to her. Again, the narrator is pointing us to the ways in which Yahweh answers prayer and provides. Additionally,

---
20   Wilch, 197.

Ruth asks in a very clever way why Boaz has noticed her; according to one commentary, the verb translated as "take notice of" or "notice" is *nakar,* and the word for "foreigner" is derived from the same root, *nakriyya.*[21] Wilch notes that the verb form is stretched a bit to make the common root clearer and create word play, which leads to alliteration in the Hebrew.[22] Ruth is saying that although she is a stranger and would normally go unnoticed—her social status—Boaz has chosen to notice her and treat her as more than a foreigner.

Ruth's question is a good one. She recognizes that as a foreigner, and not a sojourner, she would not necessarily be granted covenant privileges. A sojourner is someone who lived among other people for a long time (Wilch points out that another more legal term for understanding this would be "resident alien").[23] A foreigner is someone who is not a part of the community in any way or who has not lived among them or does not plan to live among them for an extended period. Ruth, though she plans to live with Naomi and make her life there as would a sojourner, is newly arrived; therefore, she self-identifies as a foreigner. Two verses in Deuteronomy make this distinction between a foreigner and a sojourner:

- Deuteronomy 14:21: "'You shall not eat anything that has died naturally. You may give it to the sojourner who is within your towns, that he may eat it, or you may sell it to a foreigner. For you are a people holy to the LORD your God. 'You shall not boil a young goat in its mother's milk.'" (Notice the distinction between the sojourner and the foreigner; they are to give the animal to the sojourner, but sell it to the foreigner.)

- Deuteronomy 23:20: "You may charge a foreigner interest, but you may not charge your brother interest, that the LORD your God may bless you in all that you undertake in the land that you are entering to take possession of it." (Foreigners, again, are treated differently than those who are a part of God's covenant people.)

---

21   Wilch, 199.

22   Ibid., 199.

23   Ibid., 218–9

It is clear that Boaz does not have a strong law-based obligation to Ruth, yet he has chosen to be of help to her and take notice of her. Ruth acknowledges this and is grateful.

> **The Blessings of Ruth:** As noted previously, the Book of Ruth contains several blessings spoken by different people. These blessings are important in showing how Yahweh works to answer the prayers of His faithful people, and the blessings always confess Yahweh as the one who can answer such prayers. This shows that although Yahweh seems to be in the background of the narrative, He is actually very active, and His people confess His activity in their lives by going to Him for all of their needs. Here is a list of blessings and prayers in Ruth, along with who asks the blessing and for whom:
>
> | | |
> |---|---|
> | Naomi for Ruth and Orpah: | Ruth 1:8–9 |
> | Boaz for Ruth: | Ruth 2:12 |
> | Naomi for Boaz: | Ruth 2:20 |
> | Boaz for Ruth: | Ruth 3:10 |
> | The Crowd at the Gate for Boaz: | Ruth 4:11–12 |
> | The Women for Naomi: | Ruth 4:14–15 |
>
> All of the blessings in Ruth are important to both the immediate narrative and to the ongoing history of God's work of salvation.

In response to Ruth's question, Boaz notes that he has heard of her kindness to Naomi and he asks a blessing on Ruth. Like Naomi, Boaz prays in the covenant name of God that a foreigner be blessed. (Boaz's blessing is significant to the narrative. Later, in chapter 3, Ruth draws on the language of his prayer when asking him for further help.) Boaz asks that Yahweh bless Ruth by giving her the "reward of Yahweh." This echoes language from the Genesis account of Israel's ancestors: "After these things the word of the LORD came to Abram in a vision: 'Fear not, Abram, I am your shield; your reward shall be very great'" (Genesis 15:1). Here, Yahweh promises His reward to Abram, the father of all Israel. By asking that Ruth receive the reward of Yahweh, Boaz links Ruth to the patriarchs and the matriarchs. This is important because it is through the matriarchs and the patriarchs that God's promised Seed will come. Boaz also notes that Ruth has come under Yahweh's "wings" for safety and protection. (This metaphor of the protection of Yahweh being likened to "wings" also occurs in Psalm 91:4: "He will cover you with His pinions, and under His wings you will find refuge; His faithfulness is a shield and buckler.") Such language, again, would be known to Yahweh's covenant people. Both Boaz and Naomi continually include Ruth in this language, and although she is a Moabite, her confession of the name of Yahweh has made her a part of the covenant people, because it is the gift of His name that makes His people His.

Ruth's response in the original language is better translated as "maidservant." A maidservant is a member of the household, a servant of the master. Ruth is saying that Boaz treats her as if she is a member of his household, although a lowly one. Boaz also treats her as if she is a member of the household of God despite her ethnicity.

Boaz's abundant generosity continues as he includes Ruth in the noon meal reserved for his paid workers and household servants. Indeed, he even makes sure that she eats her fill with enough left over to take to Naomi (v. 18). Additionally, Boaz commands his workers to let Ruth glean among the sheaves, in other words, in a more advantageous position. He even tells them to pull some out and leave it behind on purpose for her.

Such generosity is striking in its above-and-beyond quality. The specific laws regarding the harvest do not require so much generosity or care. They provide only for the minimum amount to keep a person alive. Due to Boaz's generosity, the narrator tells us that Ruth is able to glean thirty to fifty pounds of barley, much more than the minimum. The amazing amount prompts Naomi to ask another blessing, this one for Boaz. Naomi asks that Yahweh bless Boaz, noting that in His kindness, Yahweh has not forsaken either the dead or the living. This is a major shift in her earlier feelings and reveals how Yahweh is working also in Naomi to take away her bitterness. It also reiterates Naomi's faith that Yahweh is ultimately responsible for all things. Even Boaz's generosity is attributable only to Yahweh.

Here Naomi reveals an important detail concerning Boaz: He is a "kinsman-redeemer" or simply "redeemer." The Hebrew word here, *go'el*, is commonly translated in both ways. A *go'el* must be a family member, and his duties were these:

1. Receive a payment of restitution that accompanies a guilt offering in the event of the death of a relative to whom it was due.

2. Carry out vengeance for a murdered family member (Numbers 35:19).

3. Purchase a relative out of slavery to a non-Israelite (Leviticus 25:47–49).

4. Purchase family property that had been sold outside of the family due to poverty (Leviticus 25:24–25).[24]

The kinsman-redeemer's important duty with regard to the Book of Ruth is that of buying back family land. Naomi no longer has rights to Elimelech's land, which had been sold or leased due to the famine and their sojourn outside of Israel. The land and its yield could provide for her needs, but it won't be returned to the family until the Year of Jubilee (every fifty years). Naomi's needs are immediate; she cannot wait for the Year of Jubilee, however far off it may be. And Boaz can purchase the land on Naomi's behalf as a "redeemer," her nearest kinsman.

Naomi also tells Ruth to continue gleaning in Boaz's field. The barley harvest lasts about seven weeks, so Ruth remains in Boaz's field for about that length of time, since we know that she and Naomi arrived at about the beginning of the harvest. This period of time would have given Boaz the opportunity to observe Ruth more. At the end of chapter 2, we are left with the impression of Boaz as an important figure in Ruth and Naomi's possible recovery, and with the knowledge that, for at least seven weeks, Yahweh provided for Ruth and Naomi through the barley harvest.

DISCUSSION OF TYPE SCENES

When interpreting Ruth (as well as other narratives in the Bible such as Genesis and Exodus), it is helpful to know some conventions that are used in the writing. Conventions help us to better understand the narrator's themes and motives, which are inspired by the Holy Spirit. In other words, understanding and investigating how things are written helps us to better understand the meaning of what we are reading.

---

24   Word Biblical Commentary, 136-137.

The Book of Ruth makes use of some type-scenes, which are important in narrative. A type-scene is a scene that follows a certain structure. That structure is taken from real life (i.e., it follows how that event typically took place) and is used to order the events. Type-scenes have conventions surrounding them that would have been familiar to the audience; the audience would have known how the scene should progress and what characters should be involved. Deviations from the type-scene signal something important about the story and the people in it. You might compare this, for example, to the convention in romantic comedy films called the "meet cute." The meet cute is the moment when the two potential lovers meet for the first time. This meeting is usually accidental and often includes some sort of misunderstanding that colors the rest of the film until the characters resolve the misunderstanding and fall in love. The way the meet cute occurs often gives the viewer an idea of the personalities of the main characters. As demonstrated by conventions like the meet cute, we develop ways of understanding how our lives unfold, and these ways of understanding are often reflected in literature and film.

The Book of Ruth is a true account of true events for which a type-scene is used to help us understand the meaning of those events. Robert Alter, a Jewish scholar, has identified several different type-scenes in the biblical narratives of the Old Testament. These include:

1. Epiphany in a Field

2. Initiatory Trial (for instance, David and Goliath)

3. Betrothal (for example, an encounter with the future betrothed at a well). See the discussion below.

4. Annunciation (see for instance, Judges 13:2–7)

5. Danger in the Desert and Discovery of Well/Source of Sustenance (for example, Hagar in Genesis 16:6–15 and 21:8–21)

6. Testament of the Dying Hero (see for instance, Isaac in Genesis 27:18–45)[25]

---

25   Alter only explores Old Testament examples of this for obvious reasons. However, as Christians, we can see that Jesus fulfills even these literary conventions and these events in the lives of the Old Testament people with his life and death. Some very obvious examples should come to mind, such as the annunciation of His birth to Mary by the angel Gabriel. From: Alter, Robert, *The Art of Biblical Narrative* (New York, Basic Books, 1981).

The specific type-scene at work in this chapter of Ruth is a betrothal. To get a feel for a more typical betrothal type-scene, it is helpful to take a close look first at Genesis 29:1–20:

> Then Jacob went on his journey and came to the land of the people of the east. As he looked, he saw a well in the field, and behold, three flocks of sheep lying beside it, for out of that well the flocks were watered. The stone on the well's mouth was large, and when all the flocks were gathered there, the shepherds would roll the stone from the mouth of the well and water the sheep, and put the stone back in its place over the mouth of the well.
>
> Jacob said to them, "My brothers, where do you come from?" They said, "We are from Haran." He said to them, "Do you know Laban the son of Nahor?" They said, "We know him." He said to them, "Is it well with him?" They said, "It is well; and see, Rachel his daughter is coming with the sheep!" He said, "Behold, it is still high day; it is not time for the livestock to be gathered together. Water the sheep and go, pasture them." But they said, "We cannot until all the flocks are gathered together and the stone is rolled from the mouth of the well; then we water the sheep."
>
> While he was still speaking with them, Rachel came with her father's sheep, for she was a shepherdess. Now as soon as Jacob saw Rachel the daughter of Laban his mother's brother, and the sheep of Laban his mother's brother, Jacob came near and rolled the stone from the well's mouth and watered the flock of Laban his mother's brother. Then Jacob kissed Rachel and wept aloud. And Jacob told Rachel that he was her father's kinsman, and that he was Rebekah's son, and she ran and told her father.
>
> As soon as Laban heard the news about Jacob, his sister's son, he ran to meet him and embraced him and kissed him and brought him to his house. Jacob told Laban all these things, and Laban said to him, "Surely you are my bone and my flesh!" And he stayed with him a month.
>
> Then Laban said to Jacob, "Because you are my kinsman, should you therefore serve me for nothing? Tell me, what shall your wages be?" Now Laban had two daughters. The name of the older was Leah, and the name of the younger was Rachel. Leah's eyes were weak, but Rachel was beautiful in form and appearance. Jacob loved Rachel. And he said, "I will serve you seven years for your younger daughter Rachel." Laban said, "It is better that I give her to you than that I should give her to any other man; stay with me." So Jacob served seven years for Rachel, and they seemed to him but a few days because of the love he had for her.

In this type-scene, Jacob journeys to a foreign land, meets Rachel at the well, and helps her draw water. She then returns to her family to tell them of his arrival, and Jacob is invited to stay with them. Eventually, a betrothal is arranged. This is a fairly typical betrothal type-scene, although it includes some variations. For instance, the marriage is not immediate. Jacob is made to serve seven years for Rachel (and then, of course, Laban tricks him). Nevertheless, the key parts of the betrothal type-scene are present:

1. The future bridegroom or his surrogate journeys to a foreign land.

2. He encounters a girl or a young woman (usually the term *na'arah*, meaning "young woman," is used unless she is named).

3. Someone draws water from the well (either the hero or the woman).

4. Then the girl/girls rush home to tell of the stranger's arrival.

5. A betrothal is arranged between the two, often after he is invited to a meal.[26]

In chapter 2, the narrator of Ruth alludes to the betrothal type-scene; he is foreshadowing what is to come. This is important because a type-scene attaches the moment it captures to the larger pattern of historical and theological meaning.[27] In other words, a type-scene takes what would otherwise be an isolated event and sets it within the wider history and theology of what God is doing to bring about His purposes. Many of the patriarchs are given a betrothal type-scene (for instance Isaac, Jacob, and Moses). By using a type-scene, the narrator is connecting Ruth to the larger history of the Hebrews or the Israelites, God's chosen people. Such betrothal type-scenes are used to bring together the couples who will continue the line of the promised Seed through the bearing of their children. This suggests that the Book of Ruth may also be a part of God's great design for the salvation of His people.

---

26   These steps in the type-scene are taken from Alter, 52.

27   Alter, 60.

Given the above description and the importance of this type-scene, it is helpful to note two things: which elements of the type-scene appear in Ruth and how this betrothal type-scene differs from the pattern. Many of the elements of a betrothal type-scene are present: Ruth is a foreigner who has journeyed to a foreign land, the young men are told to (and likely do) draw water from a well for her to drink, Ruth is a "young woman," there is a shared meal, and Ruth returns home to her mother-in-law to relate the day's events.

However, several events are different: rather than the male figure, a female is the one who has journeyed to a foreign land, and while her journey is alluded to here, it took place in the previous chapter. In this way, the whole Book of Ruth is like an extended betrothal type-scene. It is the young men, Boaz's workers, who are commanded to draw the water from the well, and not Ruth or Boaz (in a traditional type-scene, one of the young men would be the more likely candidate for a pairing with Ruth). No one rushes home, although Ruth reports the events to Naomi later in the chapter. The omission of the running and hurrying throws into relief how the narrator wants to focus instead on the ideas of return and rest. The shared meal is not a family meal, but the meal during the harvest with all of the workers. Finally, the betrothal is not finalized here, so the type-scene is unresolved in this chapter.

As previously mentioned, Alter notes that the variations from the pattern are important and the way things work out tells us something about the meaning, purpose, or theology of what we are reading. The use of the type-scene hints at how God might solve Ruth's and Naomi's destitution: by bringing about a marriage for Ruth. However, given the fact that the type-scenes used for the matriarchs and patriarchs highlight important theological truths, such as God's work to bring about His promises of offspring for Abraham, there is more happening here than resolution for Naomi and Ruth. In fact, Alter says that by using reversals of the type-scene, "Ruth is conceived by the author as a kind of matriarch by adoption" when Boaz makes a very pointed allusion to Abraham's sojourn.[28] In verse 11, Boaz notes that Ruth's

---

28 Ibid., 59.

story has been told to him, including "how you left your father and mother and your native land and came to a people that you did not know before." This relates closely to Yahweh's command to Abraham: "Now the LORD said to Abram, 'Go from your country and your kindred and your father's house to the land that I will show you'" (Genesis 12:1).[29] Alter further notes: "This particular allusion links her with the movement from the East to Canaan at the beginning of the patriarchal enterprise, while the whole invocation of the betrothal type-scene suggests a certain connection with the matriarchs."[30] The connection with the matriarchs and patriarchs implies that Ruth's story and her life might be inseparable from the story and the lives of all of God's chosen people, and are, indeed, necessary to all of God's people throughout all time and to His work of salvation. How it is necessary will become clear as the history unfolds.

INTERPRETATION

One word should stand out to you as the *leitwort* of this section: *glean*. The word *glean* and all of its attendant connotations help to form the theme of this section. Ruth gleans in the field for sustenance, and Boaz allows her to do so, even allowing her to glean more than what is usual. The provision in the Law for gleaning and the activity that occurs in this section show how Yahweh is at work in simple, daily things, like the harvest, to provide for and sustain His people. Furthermore, His providence and sustenance are not just for the daily life, but also for spiritual life and life eternal. His care and concern for the body is a result of His love for His people and desire that they be resurrected to glory (as Ruth confesses in chapter 1) and is coequal to His care and concern for the soul. In fact, in seeing how Yahweh cared for her bodily needs, Naomi began to again confess Yahweh's care in a positive light. In other words, through the care of the body, Yahweh also cared for Naomi's soul. The theme of this section is that Yahweh can work through very ordinary means (harvests, gleaning, people) to bring about His purposes and His salvific work for both body and soul.

29   Ibid.
30   Alter, 59.

This is Good News to us too! For God comes to us in very ordinary Means, indeed: spoken words, water, bread, and wine. These ordinary Means are used to deliver to us healing, life, and health of both body and soul.

The focus on gleaning also reminds us of how certain people in the Book of Ruth go above and beyond the letter of the Law and what it requires in care for others. Boaz, like Ruth, interprets the Law of God (here specifically with regard to gleaning) according to its spirit. The letter of the Law requires only that a little grain be left around the edges after the harvest has been completed, and it requires that this be done only for the widows, the poor, and the sojourners. But Boaz interprets the Law according to the spirit of the Law—that of care and concern for one's neighbors (and everyone is a neighbor) and their well-being, not just that they might sustain themselves, but that they might flourish and prosper. Boaz's interpretation of the Law toward Ruth is like hers toward her mother-in-law. Unlike the Israelites, who should recognize and act according to the Law gifted to them, Ruth is the one who goes above and beyond the letter of the Law to help Naomi and care for her. In chapters 1 and 2 of the Book of Ruth, Ruth is a Christ-like figure, a type of Christ. She displays the characteristic faithfulness of God and sacrifices herself for her mother-in-law.

By portraying some of the characteristics of Christ, both Ruth herself and her story prophesy about Christ analogically (by analogy). In other words, there are events and actions in Ruth that remind us of and point us forward to Christ and what He does for us. These include Ruth's and Boaz's willingness to serve others according to the spirit of the Law, for that is what Jesus did throughout His life on this earth and what He does in all of His salvific work for us.

Discussion Questions

1. What are some of the ways in which the narrator has clued us in to Yahweh at work? In what way does the "behind the scenes" work of Yahweh in Ruth offer comfort to us as Christians today in our own lives?

2. In what ways has Ruth lived according to the spirit, rather than the letter, of the Law? What about Boaz? How does this make them types of Christ?

3. When thinking through the different type-scenes and Jesus' life, can you pinpoint the events in Jesus' life that fulfill some of these scenes?

CHAPTER 4

RUTH 3: A BOLD MOVE

OPENING PRAYER: HEAVENLY FATHER, Your desire is to love and care for all of Your creation; therefore, spread Your wings over us this day and protect us in all things so that we may testify to Your love and mercy through our lives and our words, through Jesus Christ, Your Son, our Lord, who lives and reigns with You and the Holy Spirit. Amen.

Introduction to Chapter 3 of Ruth
READ RUTH 3:1–18

IN THE PREVIOUS CHAPTER, two scenes containing interactions between Ruth and Naomi acted like bookends in the chapter. In the middle of these two scenes was the highlighted portion of the chapter: the betrothal type-scene between Ruth and Boaz. By setting off the incomplete betrothal type-scene this way, the narrator helps the hearer or reader focus on God at work through the ordinary means of the harvest and people meeting one another.

In chapter 3 of Ruth, the narrator creates a similar bookending structure. Two scenes in which Ruth and Naomi discuss their situation set off and highlight the main action of this chapter: Ruth's visit to the threshing floor. Concentrated in this central section is a particular *leitwort* that was introduced by the discussion between Ruth and Naomi in Ruth 2:20–22. The *leitwort* is *redeemer/redeem*. The theme of this chapter, then, is redemption. On the surface, the focus is on who will redeem Ruth and Naomi in their immediate context—who will buy back Elimelech's land so they can be sustained by its produce. However, the narrator is also calling to mind the theological implications of the word *redeem*, for it is Yahweh who ultimately and fully will redeem Ruth and Naomi, and indeed the whole world.

VERSE BY VERSE ANALYSIS

In chapter 2, in the similar opening scene between Ruth and Naomi, it was Ruth who took the initiative. Here in chapter 3, it is Naomi who speaks first and has a plan. Naomi's awakening, so to speak, began at the end of the previous chapter when she recognized that God was responding to her physical needs through Boaz, Ruth, and the harvest. Having recognized that circumstances are favorable, Naomi is now prepared to take further action. She is prompted by a desire not for her own comfort, but for "rest" for Ruth. Naomi is no longer bitter "Mara" (Ruth 1:20) as she was upon arriving in Bethlehem. She is able now to think of Ruth and her needs and is recalling her own prayer for her daughters-in-law that they might both find rest in the houses of their husbands (1:9). Naomi tells Ruth that she must seek rest for her now by seeking a husband for her. (Again, "rest" is a covenant blessing that Naomi extends to Ruth.) And now it is Naomi who goes above and beyond the letter of the Law by understanding the gifts of Yahweh to be not just for some people, but for all people. She recognizes that these blessings can and should extend to Ruth.

Naomi points out that Boaz will be at the threshing floor winnowing the barley from the harvest. (Barley and wheat were winnowed at the end of the harvest at a communal threshing-floor.) As the harvest comes to an end, Naomi is aware that their current mode of provision is also ending, and she wants Ruth to have a more permanent source of provision.

> **Winnowing the Barley:** The threshing floor was an open-air area in the fields that was level and had been stamped down.[31] Winnowing took place in the late afternoon to dusk, because it was cooler due to wind coming in from the Mediterranean at that time.[32] The worker would take a large fork, throw the mixture of straw, chaff, and kernels into the air, and the wind would separate the pieces. The chaff would blow the furthest away, the straw landed closer, and the grain kernels, heavier than the other materials, fell back to the threshing-floor at his feet.

---

31   Keil, *Joshua, Judges, Ruth*, in Commentary on the Old Testament (Edinburg: T. and T. Clark, 1869), 484.

32   Keil, *Joshua, Judges, Ruth*, 484 and Bush, *Ruth* Word Biblical Commentary, 150.

Naomi instructs Ruth to wash and anoint herself, because Ruth, as a widow, has up to now been in mourning. In Israelite culture, a woman wore garments of widowhood while in mourning. When she changed her clothes, it signaled that her mourning period was over. There were similar practices for men with regard to mourning, as well. Also, Israelites did not often bathe since water was scarce; instead, they anointed themselves with perfumed oils. This anointing also seems to have been a common practice after a period of mourning.

- 2 Samuel 12:15b–20: "And the LORD afflicted the child that Uriah's wife bore to David, and he became sick. David therefore sought God on behalf of the child. And David fasted and went in and lay all night on the ground. And the elders of his house stood beside him, to raise him from the ground, but he would not, nor did he eat food with them. On the seventh day the child died. And the servants of David were afraid to tell him that the child was dead, for they said, 'Behold, while the child was yet alive, we spoke to him, and he did not listen to us. How then can we say to him the child is dead? He may do himself some harm.' But when David saw that his servants were whispering together, David understood that the child was dead. And David said to his servants, 'Is the child dead?' They said, 'He is dead.' Then David arose from the earth and washed and anointed himself and changed his clothes. And he went into the house of the LORD and worshiped. He then went to his own house. And when he asked, they set food before him, and he ate."

  David mourns for the child and fasts and prays while the child is sick and dying. Once the child has died, David changes out of his mourning clothes, washes, anoints himself, and worships the Lord. Here, David's time of mourning is during the illness and not afterward, because David was also repenting for his actions in taking Uriah's wife. Yet this example still shows that specific garments and actions were expected during a time of mourning, and that when those clothes were removed, the period of mourning was considered over.

- Genesis 38:14, 19: "She took off her widow's garments, and covered herself with a veil, wrapping herself up, and sat at the entrance to Enaim, which is on the road to Timnah. For she saw that Shelah was grown up, and she had not been given to him in marriage. . . . Then she arose and went away, and taking off her veil she put on the garments of her widowhood."

This is the account of Tamar, which is very interesting in its own right. Here she removes her garments of widowhood in order to trick her father-in-law into giving her offspring to perpetuate her husband's name, according to the custom of Levirate marriage, since her father-in-law did not do right by her by giving her the next son. The garments of widowhood identify her as a widow, and when she changes, Judah does not recognize her. She returns to her garments once she has tricked Judah, because her mourning period is not fully over. There is much more that can be said concerning Tamar's story, but for our purposes, it serves as an example of how the garments of widowhood were common at the time.

By telling Ruth to remove her widow's garments, Naomi is telling her it is time to move on to the next phase of her life—her widowhood is over and Ruth is still a young woman, so she is eligible for another marriage. Then Naomi tells her to go to the threshing floor and wait until Boaz has had his meal before she presents herself to him. This is probably so that he is in a favorable mood and so that she has his undivided attention. If she approaches him before the meal, he might be hungry from the day's work and wishing to eat. During the meal, he would likely be distracted by other events. Additionally, since the threshing floor was communal, they would have little ability to talk privately. For these reasons, Naomi tells Ruth to wait until after the meal.

Naomi's instructions in verse 4 sound very strange to today's readers. She tells Ruth to uncover his feet and lie down at his feet after he has fallen asleep. People often speculate about these strange instructions, but as we know that Naomi wants what is best for her daughter-in-law and is faithful to Yahweh, we know that she cannot be asking her to do anything untoward. Naomi is giving Ruth instructions to help her make a symbolic communication to Boaz regarding marriage. We will discuss more below about what this action symbolizes.

Ruth's response is immediate, trusting, and obedient. She will do all that Naomi has told her to do; she is submissive to Naomi's will and to her instructions. This reaffirms for us Ruth's willingness to serve Naomi and her respect for Naomi as her mother-in-law and as her elder.

Verses 6–15 form the main action of this portion of the narrative. These verses, again, are set off as important by the **inclusio** formed by the two scenes with Ruth and Naomi that bookend this chapter. In verse 6, the narrator breaks from the action to address the reader and summarize the ensuing scene by emphasizing Ruth's obedience. This means that Ruth's obedience and her submission to Naomi are important to the story as a whole and to understanding Ruth better.

The narrator notes that Boaz eats and drinks "until his heart was merry." This does not mean that Boaz was drunk. The Bible, in fact, often affirms the ability of wine (in moderation) to make the heart glad or merry, but it does not condone drunkenness.

Sacrificial and Celebratory Wine in Scripture: Sample passages wherein wine is referred to as a part of celebrating include:

- Exodus 29:40 and Numbers 28:14: Wine is used as part of the drink offering to Yahweh here. This is, of course, a forerunner to Christ's own drink offering: that of His blood in His sacrificial death on the cross.
- Deuteronomy 7:13: An abundance of wine is part of Yahweh's blessings, along with an abundance of other fruits of the earth.
- Psalm 104:14–15: Wine is one of the gifts of God to "gladden the heart of man."
- Proverbs 3:9–10: Vats bursting with wine are a reward to those who honor the Lord with their firstfruits.
- Ecclesiastes 9:7: Life is to be enjoyed, including drinking wine with a "merry heart."
- Ecclesiastes 10:19: Wine "gladdens life."

These examples are not exhaustive, but they do serve to show that wine can be a source of pleasure for God's people and to show its importance in the sacrificial system that was fulfilled by Christ's institution of the Lord's Supper. There are also many verses about the evils of drunkenness, but the verses listed here refer to the gift of God that wine, like the other fruits of the earth, is. Like the other gifts of God, it can be misused, but that is a result of our sin. Here, Boaz drinks until he is merry, because God has abundantly blessed the harvest and they are celebrating His gifts.

This also would have been a typical end to the day of threshing. After their work was done, the men would eat a meal and drink wine. Wine was often consumed to celebrate the harvest as a sign of abundance, though not to the point of drunkenness (see the sidebar). The owners would then sleep near their harvest at the threshing floor to guard it, since it was a communal threshing floor.

The conditions are now as Naomi would have them be for Ruth to make her bold move. In verse 7, she quietly goes to Boaz, uncovers his feet, and lies down. Ruth does not uncover Boaz's feet too far up his leg, as is evidenced by the Hebrew word used for the bottom part of the leg and the foot. Although the word is sometimes used as a euphemism for the male genitalia, that is not its formal meaning. This, in combination with other subtle euphemisms in the Hebrew with regard to the words for "lie" and "know" (both used in the Old Testament when a husband has intercourse with his wife), leads some to think that Ruth's action was a sexual proposition. However, as we will see, her action is a symbolic gesture, probably a gesture of humility. Horace D. Hummel, in his introduction to the Old Testament[33], notes that such subtle word play highlights how covenant people act in situations of temptation. He notes that: "the temptation to premature coitus is highlighted as much as it is precisely to stress that this is *not* the response of covenanted people who live within the context of *chesedh*. It is surely no accident that Boaz praises Ruth (3:10) for that very quality as he agrees to pursue the matter promptly."[34] This issue must be addressed, as people do make assumptions about what happened in this portion of the narrative. There are those who believe that Ruth enticed Boaz. However, knowing as we do that they both are faithful, covenantal people declared by the narrator to be "worthy," we

33 Horace D. Hummel, *The Word Becoming Flesh: An Introduction to the Origin, Purpose, and Meaning of the Old Testament* (St. Louis: Concordia, 1979), 506–516.

34 Horace D. Hummel, *The Word Becoming Flesh*, 513. Italics are in the original.

know that while the possibility of sexual sin is there, neither of them act upon it. This serves to further show us that both Ruth and Boaz are worthy, faithful people.

Boaz discovers Ruth when he turns over and feels someone at his feet. When he asks who is there, Ruth identifies herself as his "servant" (ESV). However, this is not the same word used in 2:13, where Ruth also refers to herself as his servant. There the word translated as "servant" was really "maidservant." Here the word is better translated as "handmaiden," and Ruth's word choice acknowledges that Boaz has shown her more kindness and import than he would a mere maidservant. A handmaiden was eligible to marry a slave or to be the concubine of a free man and was ranked higher socially, though still not a free person herself. Therefore, Ruth is still showing a great deal of humility by calling herself a "handmaiden" and not a "woman."[35]

Ruth asks Boaz to "spread his wings" over her because of his status as a redeemer (see the discussion of what a redeemer can do on page 73 in chapter 3). The word translated as "wings" is also used in Boaz's blessing and prayer for Ruth, where he notes that she has come to Israel to take refuge under Yahweh's wings (2:12). The word can also refer to the corners of a garment. This same idea shows up in Ezekiel 16:8, where Yahweh is speaking about Israel. Yahweh says, "When I passed by you again and saw you, behold, you were at the age for love, and I spread the corner of My garment over you and covered your nakedness; I made My vow to you and entered into a covenant with you, declares the Lord GOD, and you became Mine." Given this understanding of the word used for "wings," it becomes clear that Ruth's uncovering of Boaz's feet, which required her to open up his garment, was a symbolic gesture asking him to use his garment—his wings—to cover her by marrying her. This goes back to the unfinished type-scene in chapter 2, as a marriage is finally proposed (though still not concluded). Here again, though, the events of Ruth's life differ in significant ways from the typical betrothal scene, as she, the woman, makes the proposal of marriage rather than the man.

---

35   Wilch, 285.

As these verses demonstrate, the imagery of taking refuge under Yahweh's wings is a prevalent one in Scripture, so to the believing reader, Ruth's request of Boaz is not so strange. It trusts that Boaz, like Yahweh, is gracious and longs to spread his wings over his servants to shelter and save them.

Boaz responds by again asking that Ruth be blessed by Yahweh. Her behavior—going to him rather than pursuing younger men—is a "kindness" and a commendation of her sincerity and honor. The word translated here as "kindness" is again the Hebrew word *chesed* (this is the verse to which Hummel points in his quotation above). This word can also be translated and understood as "faithfulness." Ruth shows faithfulness to Naomi by pursuing an arrangement that helps Naomi regain her land and, perhaps, provides an heir for Elimelech and Naomi's family. Ruth is also faithful to Yahweh in living a life of service and submission to her neighbor, Naomi.

Boaz's words also offer insight into their relative ages. It is clear that Boaz is older than Ruth. There are other clues to Boaz's age, as well. Dialogue in biblical literature often reveals differences between characters. Both Naomi and Boaz use an archaic construction in the Hebrew called a paragogic nun (an extra *n* at the end of certain Hebrew words). Although it is impossible to adequately translate into English the differences in their speech, this Hebrew construction tells us that Naomi and Boaz are about the same age and, therefore, that Boaz is older than Ruth. This also implies that Boaz probably already has one wife, according to normal Hebrew conventions. Boaz promises to do everything he can for Ruth, because he knows that she is a "worthy" woman. The narrator used "worthy" (the same Hebrew word) to refer to Boaz in Ruth 2:1. In this way, Ruth and Boaz are similar.

Things are going well with Naomi's plan, but Boaz has one surprise for us for which even the narrator has not prepared us: there is a "nearer redeemer," a closer relative who has the first right and duty of redemption. Yahweh commands this duty in Leviticus 25:25: "If your brother becomes poor and sells part of his property, then his nearest redeemer shall come and redeem what his brother has sold." It may be that Naomi had previous knowledge of this nearer redeemer, but chose to go to Boaz anyway since he had shown them kindness and generosity during the harvest; however, we cannot know for sure how much Naomi knew about the other relative. After giving Ruth this information, Boaz instructs her to remain for the night. This is probably a means of protecting her, as traveling alone at night was not safe. He does, however, promise that he will redeem her if the other man will not. This is a certain promise as he swears an oath by the name of Yahweh. It is clear that he intends to do all that he can to help Ruth.

Boaz sends Ruth home in the early morning, before she can be recognized, in order to protect her reputation. There is nothing to hide with regard to their behavior, but the fact that she was at the threshing floor during the night could give a wrong impression. Before he sends her home, he gives her six measures of barley to take with her. Boaz's gift and Ruth's return to the city end this section, which is the main event of this chapter. Again, the *leitwort* of this section has been *redeem*. Not only do Ruth and Naomi long for redemption, and not only does Boaz offer to redeem them in the here and now, Yahweh is working out greater kinds of redemption that have yet to be revealed.

The narrator then returns to a scene between Ruth and Naomi, as has been a central motif of the entire Book of Ruth. Here Ruth reports to Naomi all that happened, including what Boaz said to her before they parted. She reports that he gave her the six measures of barley so she will not return home to her mother-in-law "empty-handed." Boaz's use of this term echoes the fact that Ruth and Naomi returned to Israel "empty" of all things—both family and daily provision. Yet, Yahweh has continuously worked to "fill" them in the category of daily provision through Boaz and the barley harvest. Boaz's promise of continued help and his provision point to the fact that Yahweh is also working to fill the other aspect of their emptiness by providing a family and a source of constant care for them.

Naomi has final instructions for Ruth: Now it is time for them to cease doing and wait on Boaz's actions. This is because Boaz, as a man, can work this transaction for them and because, as a worthy man, he can be trusted to do so to their benefit. Naomi knows that Boaz will not rest until he has settled everything on their behalf.

INTERPRETATION

This chapter of Ruth is rich for further interpretation. As a pivotal point in this true story, chapter 3 touches on many of the main themes of the Book of Ruth. There are a few key points that are especially worth noting: Ruth's Christlike submission, the theme of redemption, Yahweh's wings, and the theme of waiting on the Lord.

RUTH'S CHRISTLIKE SUBMISSION

In Ruth's submission to both the will of Naomi and the will of Boaz, we see the kind of submission to the will of God the Father that Christ demonstrates. Ruth must be aware that what Naomi has asked of her includes some risk. Her reputation could be damaged or destroyed by her visit to the threshing floor at night and in secret. Her proposal to Boaz, for that is what her actions will constitute, could be rejected; he might see something improper in it or choose not to help them in that way. Because she is a foreigner, the loss of Ruth's reputation as a result of such actions would be devastating and could harm her prospects forever. Additionally, if Boaz and Ruth were thought to have engaged in a sexual relationship, they could both be put to death (see for instance, Leviticus 20:10 and Deuteronomy 22:13–30). Despite these risks, Ruth submits to Naomi's will to visit Boaz and propose marriage to him. Likewise, she submits to Boaz's instructions to lie at his feet until the morning, return to the city before dawn, and wait for him to settle matters with the nearer redeemer.

In her submission and humility and other Christlike characteristics, Ruth is a type of Christ. When faced with His certain suffering and death, Jesus submits to the Father's will for Him, praying, "My Father, if this cannot pass unless I drink it, Your will be done" (Matthew 26:42b). Jesus then meets His Father's will boldly and head on, saying to His disciples, "Rise, let us be going, see My betrayer is at hand" (Matthew 26:46). He submits fully to the Father's will, although He knows it will bring death and separation from the Father. As St. Paul so eloquently puts it in his Letter to the Philippians: "[Jesus], though He was in the form of God, did not count equality with God a thing to be grasped, but emptied Himself, by taking the form of a servant, being born in the likeness of men. And being found in human form, He humbled Himself by becoming obedient to the point of death, even death on a cross" (Philippians 2:6–8).

REDEMPTION

As previously noted, the *leitwort* of chapter 3 of Ruth is *redeem*. This word points to the very practical and immediate concern of redeeming

Elimelech's land for Naomi and Ruth. Through such a redemption, Boaz (and Yahweh) can provide for Ruth and Naomi for many years to come, as they will be able to live off of the proceeds of the land. By buying back the land, Boaz will secure Ruth and Naomi's earthly lives. Both Ruth and Naomi seek this redemption, and both trust that Boaz will act to redeem the land on their behalf. This centers on the idea of the kinsman-redeemer, a part of God's Law. Yahweh Himself provides the means for His people to be redeemed from slavery and poverty in their earthly lives by a relative who acts on their behalf. To *redeem* is to "buy back," and this is what the human kinsman-redeemer literally does—he buys back his relative from slavery, or he buys back his relative's portion of the Promised Land so that it may continue in the family.

{ *Some Key Old Testament Passages on "Redeem/Redeemer/Redemption"* }

Besides those covered in the text here, there are many more passages in Scripture that deal with redemption. Here are a few key ones from the Old Testament:

- 2 Samuel 7:23
- Psalm 19:14
- Psalm 107:1–3
- Job 19:25
- Jeremiah 31:11
- Lamentations 3:58
- Micah 4:10

This is not an exhaustive list of the occurrences of this word in Scripture, but these passages are a good sample of the richness of this theme.

The theme of redemption also points forward analogically to God's overall act of redemption in Christ Jesus. His constant work is the redemption of His people. God Himself performs the first right of redemption for His people. He is the kinsman-redeemer *par excellence.* Just as the kinsman-redeemer is charged with buying a relative out of slavery, so Yahweh has bought His people out of slavery: "Say therefore to the people of Israel, 'I am the LORD, and I will bring you out from under the burdens of the Egyptians, and I will deliver you from slavery to them, and I will redeem you with an outstretched arm and with great acts of judgment'" (Exodus 6:6). The Lord's redemption of His people becomes a part of how they know themselves: "You have led in Your steadfast love the people whom You have redeemed; You have guided them by Your strength to Your holy abode" (Exodus 15:13). Here, Moses and the Israelites identify themselves as Yahweh's redeemed people. His redemption stamps them as His and leads to their ability to enter into His "holy abode."

One of the titles with which the Israelites associate Yahweh is "Redeemer" (for instance, see Job 19:25). Isaiah confesses that "Our Redeemer—the LORD of hosts is His name—is the Holy One of Israel" (Isaiah 47:4). Again, Isaiah testifies: "For your Maker is your husband, the LORD of hosts is His name; and the Holy One of Israel is your Redeemer, the God of the whole earth He is called" (54:5). Throughout the Old Testament, Yahweh as the Redeemer is confessed. The Scriptures confess that He has redeemed His people in the past, does so in the present, and will do so in the future. Therefore it follows that the use of the word *redeem* throughout this section of Ruth should remind readers of the kind of Redeemer that Yahweh is: the kind who promises to save His people from sin (Genesis 3:15 is the first instance of this promise), who brings His people out of slavery in Egypt, and who gives them the Promised Land. Of course, the future promise of Yahweh's redemption is also at work here, but to see how Ruth connects to that promise, we must keep reading!

YAHWEH'S WINGS

As discussed, Ruth's lifting up of the corner of Boaz's garment is a symbolic gesture asking for his help and protection and is linked to the idea of "spreading one's wings" over another person. This simple action is a theologically rich one. In it, Ruth references Yahweh's own action in that He has done this very thing for His people, Israel. Remember that the Hebrew word for "wings" can also refer to the "corners of a garment." This is why Ruth's action of turning back Boaz's garment is a symbolic gesture. Throughout the Old Testament, the Hebrew people are seen collectively as Yahweh's Bride, and Yahweh is seen as the Bridegroom. This is the entire theme of the Book of Hosea, where Hosea's life becomes an object lesson comparing his marriage to a prostitute to Yahweh's faithfulness to His Bride, Israel, who whores after other gods, such as Ba'al. One place where this is beautifully pictured is in Ezekiel: "When I passed by you again and saw you, behold, you were at the age for love, and I spread the **corner of my garment** over you and covered your nakedness; I made My vow to you and entered into a covenant with you, declares the Lord GOD, and you became Mine" (16:8). This is the same phrase that is used in Ruth's request of Boaz in 3:9. Yahweh spreads the wings or corners of His garment over His people, covering their nakedness and taking them as His Bride. The metaphor of Yahweh taking Israel as His Bride and gathering His people to Himself is used often throughout the Old Testament.

Like the hen referenced by Jesus (Matthew 23:37–38), God gathers us around Word and Sacrament—indeed around Christ Himself—and spreads His wings over us through the Church here on earth. Even if it seems to us that God's presence is missing from other areas of our lives, in the Church we find that He is still spreading His wings over us, covering our nakedness, and making us into His Bride. By using this metaphor in regard to Boaz, the narrator shows us that Boaz is also a type of Christ. Like Yahweh, like Christ, Boaz will spread his wings over his servant, Ruth, to save her and redeem her.

EMPTINESS AND FULLNESS

In this chapter, the theme of emptiness and fullness resurfaces. Throughout the Book of Ruth, Yahweh is working to fill the emptiness of Ruth and Naomi. This "filling" comes in the form of filling their stomachs through the barley harvest with what is needed to sustain life. This provision foreshadows His future provision and is a reminder that God does provide for our needs. When Naomi returns to Bethlehem, she is bereft of food, money, land, husband, and children. In chapter 1 of Ruth, Yahweh is poised to fill Naomi's emptiness through Ruth. In chapter 2, Yahweh begins to fill that emptiness through Ruth's work in the fields and Boaz's generosity. By the end of the chapter, Naomi is able to see that Yahweh has been providing for them, and she thanks Him for Boaz and pronounces a blessing on "the man who took notice of you" (Ruth 2:19).

Here in chapter 3, Yahweh is poised to fill Naomi's emptiness in more than one way. Through Boaz as the redeemer, God fulfills Naomi's emptiness of land and family. This is shown in Ruth's report of Boaz's words—"You must not go back empty-handed to your mother-in-law" (Ruth 3:17)—as he weighs Ruth down with yet more barley. The food also serves as a guarantee of sorts of Boaz's promise to work on their behalf to redeem Elimelech's land. In chapter 4, Yahweh, through Ruth and Boaz, will fill Naomi's emptiness full to overflowing. And He does the same for us, as we will see.

Discussion Questions

1. Ruth's garments of widowhood and the Israelites' traditions for periods of mourning indicate to others, even strangers, that she is mourning. It also gives her a marked time period to publicly grieve. Often, this period was at least one year long. How do we mark our losses in our society today? How is it sufficient or insufficient? Do you think there might have been something helpful about the traditions of the Israelites? What are some ways that, even without garments of mourning to remind us, we can enter into the grieving of our friends and remember their losses over an extended period of time?

2. Think of a time when you have been empty and Yahweh has filled you. In what way were you empty? How did He fill you? How does He fill us each and every Sunday?

3. If someone asked you, "Where is Yahweh in the Book of Ruth?" how would you answer them so far?

4. Is Boaz, as the "redeemer" of Naomi and Ruth, also a type of Christ? What characteristics or actions of Boaz point forward to Christ so far in the Book of Ruth?

5. If you had to pinpoint a strong theological theme in this section based on the text, themes with which you are familiar, and our discussion, what would it be? What does it tell us about Yahweh?

CHAPTER 5

DISCUSSION OF RUTH AND PROVERBS 31:10–31

OPENING PRAYER: LORD JESUS CHRIST, you are
the Wisdom from above. Give us the wisdom that fears
the Lord and clings to You so that we may at last attain
the life, forgiveness, salvation, and resurrection that You
have promised to us, for You live and reign with the Father
and the Holy Spirit, one God, now and forever. Amen.

Introduction

AS CHAPTER 3 OF THE BOOK OF RUTH comes to a close, Ruth fades
into the background of the main action of the story. Before we turn to
chapter 4, where Boaz takes center stage, there is more for us to learn
about Ruth and her significance as a type of Christ. As has been discussed previously in our study, the word *worthy* is used to describe both
Boaz and Ruth. The word choice is no accident; the narrator is not using it haphazardly. As we know, the narrator is purposeful in all that he
does. His word choices reveal how God is at work in Ruth and beyond.

The narrator's word choice connects directly to Proverbs 31:10–31,
where the same word used in Ruth to describe her as "worthy" is also
used of the woman of Proverbs 31. Therefore, Ruth and the woman of
Proverbs 31:10–31 are connected. When studied together, they shed
light on one another. Proverbs 31:10–31 is well-known. It is also a text
that can be seen in many different ways. Sometimes it is done well, but
other times it can be used or understood as Law. In both cases, it is very
often read apart from its larger context, which means that there is more
to learn about this oft-quoted proverb.

BRIEF BACKGROUND ON PROVERBS[36]

The proverbs are all linked together, but can be misunderstood if they are taken separately and in isolation. Many parts of Proverbs are attributed to a specific author. Proverbs 31:1–9 is attributed to King Lemuel; other authors are Solomon, "wise men," and Agur. Proverbs 31:10–31 is not attributed,[37] although it may have also been written by King Lemuel.[38] In Proverbs 1–9, two women are contrasted: Lady Wisdom and Dame Folly. The rest of Proverbs is tied to these two personas. Either we are on the path of Lady Wisdom (the path of Yahweh) or the path of Dame Folly (other gods). Proverbs 10–31 contains the shorter sayings most people think of when they think of proverbs. Yet even these should be read in the light of the long discourses on wisdom in chapters 1–9 (with chapter 8 as the sort of high point of the explication of Lady Wisdom). The fear of Yahweh is the determining factor in whether a person is following after Lady Wisdom or Dame Folly. The shorter proverbs are not absolute, nor are they always true. They are generally true sayings that should be read in the light of the first nine chapters and their depiction of Lady Wisdom versus Dame Folly.

Lady Wisdom leads to life, and Dame Folly leads to death. This dichotomy is set up early in the book when Wisdom is introduced: "Wisdom cries aloud in the street, in the markets she raises her voice; at the head of the noisy streets she cries out; at the entrance of the city gates she speaks: 'How long, O simple ones, will you love being simple? How long will scoffers delight in their scoffing and fools hate knowledge? . . . For the simple are killed by their turning away and the complacency of fools destroys them; but whoever listens to me will dwell secure and will be at ease, without dread of disaster'" (Proverbs 1:20–22, 32–33). The way of Lady Wisdom leads to life, and to ignore her and enter into her counterpart's home leads to death.

---

36 For these insights into the overall drive of the Book of Proverbs, I am indebted to the course handbook for my Psalms and Writings course (EO–106, Psalms and Writings, Spring '05–'06) by Rev. Dr. R. Reed Lessing at Concordia Seminary, St. Louis, MO, 2005), 18–26. And Raymond B. Dillard and Tremper Longman III, *An Introduction to the Old Testament* (Grand Rapids, MI: Zondervan, 1994), 235–245.

37 Dillard and Longman, *An Introduction to the Old Testament,* 236.

38 Lessing, Psalms and Writings, 20.

Dame Folly is personified as the wicked woman, and to go in to her is death:

> The woman Folly is loud;
> she is seductive and knows nothing.
> She sits at the door of her house;
> she takes a seat on the highest places of the town,
> calling to those who pass by,
> who are going straight on their way,
> "Whoever is simple, let him turn in here!"
> And to him who lacks sense she says,
> "Stolen water is sweet,
> and bread eaten in secret is pleasant."
> But he does not know that the dead are there,
> that her guests are in the depths of Sheol. (Proverbs 9:13–18)

Here the distinction is clear: Lady Wisdom equals life; Dame Folly equals death. Lady Wisdom calls to those who are lost and invites them to come in and partake of her wisdom, which is sustenance for life. Dame Folly steals the food she offers, and going to her leads to death. Lady Wisdom comes from and points to Yahweh. Dame Folly is associated with Baalism and death.[39] This is the backdrop against which Proverbs 8 and Proverbs 31:10–31 should be read, even as we read them in conjunction with the Book of Ruth.

THE CONNECTION BETWEEN RUTH AND PROVERBS 31:10–31

As noted in chapter 1, the Book of Ruth, as one of the Writings, was grouped with other Writings like Psalms and Proverbs. While our English Bibles place Ruth after Judges because they are chronologically related, the Hebrew Bible placed Ruth after Proverbs. This seems like a random choice, but it was actually deliberate. As mentioned above, the word for "worthy" occurs in Proverbs 31:10–31. Here it may also be translated as "strength." The subtitle that editors usually choose for this section is "A Worthy Woman" or "The Woman Who Fears the Lord" (subtitles, chapters, verses, and headings were not in the original documents). By placing the Book of Proverbs and the Book of Ruth together, the original compilers were making a point: Proverbs

---

39   For a simple overview of this distinction, see Dillard and Longman, 242–44.

31:10–31 and Ruth are related. Besides the fact that both Ruth and the woman of Proverbs 31:10–31 are called "worthy" women, they have other similarities. Read Proverbs 31:10–31.

It should be apparent that the woman of Proverbs 31:10–31 is diligent, hardworking, and a self-starter. She does whatever it takes to care for her family. She is also faithful to Yahweh, supportive of her family, self-sacrificial, and loving. Just by noticing these characteristics in a quick read-through, it is clear that Ruth and the woman of Proverbs 31:10–31 have much in common. In fact, Ruth is a model of the woman of Proverbs 31, and the narrator wants her to be seen in this way.[40] Both the narrator of Ruth, who places a focus on Ruth as "worthy," and the arrangers of the Hebrew canon seem to want us to come to this conclusion. Ruth works tirelessly for Naomi, she is "worthy" or "strong," she is industrious and self-sacrificial, but most of all, she is faithful to Yahweh. Ruth displays the "fear of the Lord"; that is the highest praise given to the woman of Proverbs 31. She honors Yahweh as He should be honored and lives according to His Law and His grace. This strong connection between Ruth and the "Worthy Woman" shows how Ruth, though a foreigner, lives up to an ideal of a faithful Israelite woman. Ruth, then, belongs with the people of God despite her status as a Moabite. In Ruth's specific context, her diligence and self-sacrifice all are related to her work for Naomi. She returns with Naomi to a land that is not her own, sacrificing her family and her former beliefs; she sacrifices her energy and time by working tirelessly in the fields to sustain them; and she risks her reputation and well-being by asking Boaz to act as their kinsman-redeemer and as a Levir (one who enters into a Levirate marriage for the sake of producing an heir for a deceased brother).

PROVERBS 8 AND PROVERBS 31:10–31[41]

---

40 Wilch also notes this close connection in his commentary. See Wilch, 292–3. It is a fairly traditional connection made by many scholars and even those writing overviews of Ruth. Also see Dillard and Longman, 242.

41 In this section, I do a close study of the two texts to show how they are related to one another. This work is mine, but I was first steered in this direction by Rev. Dr. R. Reed Lessing in the spring of 2006. As I was working on the second incarnation of this Bible study for my field work, I asked Dr. Lessing for any advice. He encouraged me to look at Ruth in the light of Proverbs 31:10–31 and to read Proverbs 8. Dillard and Longman also briefly touch on the correlation between these two texts: "The book [of Proverbs] concludes with a powerful acrostic poem on the virtuous woman. This woman reflects her association with Lady Wisdom in Proverbs 8. She is capable both in the home and outside. It is intentional that in the Hebrew Bible, the book of Proverbs (and specifically Proverbs 31) is followed first by Ruth and then the Song of Songs" (242).

The connections do not end there. Proverbs 31:10–31 is closely connected to another important passage in Proverbs 8. Read Proverbs 31:10–31 and 8 together. You should notice some key words, phrases, and concepts that occur in both passages. Proverbs 31 is a description of "The Woman Who Fears the Lord" or "The Worthy Woman"; Proverbs 8 is Lady Wisdom's description of herself. Below is a chart that shows more closely the parallel concepts and ideas. I recommend reading the whole of each chapter on your own before you study the chart.

{ *Table 1: Linguistic and Subject Commonalities in Proverbs 31:10–31 and Proverbs 8* }

Concept in Common	Proverbs 31	Proverbs 8
More precious than jewels	10b: "She is far more,, precious than jewels.	10–11a: "Take my instruction instead of silver, and knowledge rather than choice gold, for wisdom is better than jewels."
Strength/Worthy (Note that this is the same Hebrew word that is used of Ruth and Boaz in the Book of Ruth.)	17: "She dresses herself with strength and makes her arms strong." 25: "Strength and dignity are her clothing, and she laughs at the time to come."	14: I have counsel and sound wisdom; I have insight; I have strength.
In the gates	23: "Her husband is known in the gates." 31b: "and let her works praise her in the gates."	3: "beside the gates in front of the town, at the entrance of the portals she cries aloud."
The words of her mouth	26: "She opens her mouth with wisdom, and the teaching of kindness is on her tongue."	6–8: "Hear, for I will speak noble things, and from my lips will come what is right, for my mouth will utter truth; wickedness is an abomination to my lips. All the words of my mouth are righteous; there is nothing twisted or crooked in them."
The fear of the Lord	30: "Charm is deceitful, and beauty is vain, but a woman who fears the LORD is to be praised."	13: "The fear of the LORD is hatred of evil."
Fruit of her labors	31a: "Give her the fruit of her hands."	19: "My fruit is better than gold, even fine gold, and my yield than choice silver."

As you compare the parallel phrases and concepts, you will notice that both speak of wisdom being better than jewels and better than fine gold or silver. Each chapter refers to "the gates." The gates of a town were where all business was transacted, where the elders sat to make judgments, and where most of public life occurred. This was because the gates were the hub of activity, used by everyone to go out to their fields and then come back into the city. It was important to be respected when you were "in the gates," because it meant that your fellow citizens saw your worth. This is also a reference to being worthy enough to sit among the elders of the town.

Both chapters focus on "the fear of Yahweh" as the most important aspect of life. The highest possible praise for the woman described in Proverbs 31:10–31 is that she fears the Lord. In Proverbs 8, "the fear of [Yahweh]" is defined and identified as the hatred of evil. Both passages refer to the fruits of labor. Proverbs 31 states that she should receive the fruit of her hands, while in Proverbs 8, the fruit of the speaker is described as being better than fine gold and choice silver. Both chapters refer to the sanctity of their speech or instruction. It should become clear that the speaker in Proverbs 8 is the same as the woman of Proverbs 31.[42] The question now is, "Who, ultimately, is this woman?"

To answer that, we have to look more closely at Proverbs 8. Proverbs 8 is written from the first person point of view, and the introduction (verses 1–3) tells us that Wisdom is being quoted. She stands beside the heights and speaks the remaining verses. These are the words of Wisdom personified. In the Hebrew, abstract nouns such as *love* and *wisdom* are in the feminine conjugation. *Wisdom* is a feminine noun and is therefore characterized in Proverbs 8 and 31 as a woman. But wisdom, biblically speaking, is more than just a concept. Wisdom is a person. Who, then, is Wisdom? Let's focus in on verses 22–31 of Proverbs 8:

---

42   Again, you can see Dillard and Longman, 242 for other scholars who make this connection.

"The LORD possessed me at the beginning of His work,
    the first of His acts of old.
Ages ago I was set up,
    at the first, before the beginning of the earth.
When there were no depths I was brought forth,
    when there were no springs abounding with water.
Before the mountains had been shaped,
    before the hills, I was brought forth,
    before He had made the earth with its fields,
        or the first of the dust of the world.
When He established the heavens, I was there;
    when He drew a circle on the face of the deep,
    when He made firm the skies above,
    when He established the fountains of the deep,
    when He assigned to the sea its limit,
        so that the waters might not transgress His command,
    when He marked out the foundations of the earth,
    then I was beside Him, like a master workman,
        and I was daily His delight,
    rejoicing before Him always,
    rejoicing in His inhabited world
        and delighting in the children of man.

These verses describe Wisdom as having been present prior to the creation: Wisdom was with the Lord at the "beginning of His work." Wisdom is like a "master workman," meaning that Wisdom participates in the act of creating the world. Wisdom is possessed by the Lord, and was set up before the creation of the world. These concepts echo other Scriptural passages:

Genesis 1: In Genesis chapter 1, the entire Trinity is present and active in the creation of the heavens and the earth. God the Father creates by speaking, through His Word. Jesus is the Word Incarnate, so He is present and active in creation. The Spirit is "hovering over the face of the waters" as well (v. 2). In this account, we also see that God refers to Himself in a plural form: "Let us make man in our image" (v. 26). The creation account very clearly shows that the triune God worked to bring about creation.

Psalm 2:7: "I will tell of the decree: The LORD said to Me, 'You are My Son; today I have begotten You.'" This is a reference to Jesus as God's only-begotten Son; as such, He was present with God from before the foundations of the world. We confess that He is the "only-begotten Son . . . begotten of His Father before all worlds" in the Nicene Creed.[43]

John 1:1–3: "In the beginning was the Word, and the Word was with God, and the Word was God. He was in the beginning with God. All things were made through Him, and without Him was not any thing made that was made."

Hebrews 1:1–2: "Long ago, at many times and in many ways, God spoke to our fathers by the prophets, but in these last days He has spoken to us by His Son, whom He appointed the heir of all things, through whom also He created the world."

Colossians 1:15–17: "[Christ] is the image of the invisible God, the firstborn of all creation. For by Him all things were created, in heaven and on earth, visible and invisible, whether thrones or dominions or rulers or authorities—all things were created through Him and for Him. And He is before all things, and in Him all things hold together." (Jesus is before all things, all things were created through Him, and He continues to sustain all of creation.)

Of course, the person referenced in these scriptural passages is Jesus Christ. Jesus is the one who was present with God from the beginning of His works, who was "brought forth" by God, and through whom the world was created. It follows then that Wisdom is Jesus and Jesus is Wisdom Incarnate.

The New Testament testifies to this truth in several places. In Matthew 11, John the Baptist, who by now is imprisoned by Herod, hears of Jesus' deeds and sends his disciples to ask, "Are You the one who is to come, or shall we look for another?" (Matthew 11:2). As an answer, Jesus lists His deeds: the lame walk, the blind see, the deaf hear, the lepers are cleansed, the dead are raised, and the poor hear the preach-

---

43   The Nicene Creed can be found in The Commission on Worship of The Lutheran Church—Missouri Synod, *Lutheran Service Book* (St. Louis: Concordia, 2006), 158.

ing of the Good News (Matthew 11:4–5). Jesus addresses the crowds concerning John the Baptist, telling them that there is no one greater than John who has been born of women. Then Jesus says,

> But to what shall I compare this generation? It is like children
> sitting in the marketplaces and calling to their playmates,
>
> "We played the flute for you, and you did not dance;
> we sang a dirge, and you did not mourn."
>
> For John came neither eating nor drinking, and they say,
> "He has a demon." The Son of Man came eating and drinking,
> and they say, "Look at Him! A glutton and a drunkard, a friend
> of tax collectors and sinners!" Yet wisdom is justified by her deeds.
> (Matthew 11:16–19)

In this verse, Jesus is referring to Himself. He is not calling Himself female, rather He is drawing attention to the Old Testament personifications of Wisdom and showing that He is the fulfillment and, indeed, He *is* Wisdom. Notice that in both Proverbs 8 and 31, many of the things that distinguish Wisdom are her deeds. Jesus' deeds point to Him as Wisdom and as the Christ. The deeds He listed in the earlier verses are those that were prophesied as deeds of the Messiah. Jesus is saying that He, Wisdom Incarnate, is the long-awaited Messiah, and that despite the objections of those who say He is a "glutton and a drunkard," His deeds will clearly show Him to be who He claims to be. Additionally, Jesus refers to Himself as Wisdom when He is chastising the Pharisees who ask Him for a sign (a ridiculous request after all that He has already done in fulfillment of the Old Testament). Jesus answers them in part by saying, "The queen of the South will rise up at the judgment with this generation and condemn it, for she came from the ends of the earth to hear the wisdom of Solomon, and behold, something greater than Solomon is here" (Matthew 12:42). By contrasting Himself with Solomon, considered to be one of the wisest men to ever live, Jesus is saying that He is wiser than Solomon. This is because Jesus is Wisdom in the flesh.

Consider also this similar passage from Luke, where Jesus pronounces judgment on the Pharisees, scribes, and lawyers who claim to know God's wisdom, but who do not recognize Jesus:

One of the lawyers answered Him, "Teacher, in saying these things you insult us also." And He said, "Woe to you lawyers also! For you load people with burdens hard to bear, and you yourselves do not touch the burdens with one of your fingers. Woe to you! For you build the tombs of the prophets whom your fathers killed. So you are witnesses and you consent to the deeds of your fathers, for they killed them, and you build their tombs. Therefore also the Wisdom of God said, 'I will send them prophets and apostles, some of whom they will kill and persecute,' so that the blood of all the prophets, shed from the foundation of the world, may be charged against this generation, from the blood of Abel to the blood of Zechariah, who perished between the altar and the sanctuary. Yes, I tell you, it will be required of this generation. Woe to you lawyers! For you have taken away the key of knowledge. You did not enter yourselves, and you hindered those who were entering." (Luke 11:45–52)

Once again, Wisdom is personified, and Jesus is referring to Himself. Paul continues this idea in his Letter to the Corinthians, where he contrasts the wisdom of the world with the wisdom of God:

For Jews demand signs and Greeks seek wisdom, but we preach Christ crucified, a stumbling block to Jews and folly to Gentiles, but to those who are called, both Jews and Greeks, Christ the power of God and the wisdom of God. For the foolishness of God is wiser than men, and the weakness of God is stronger than men.

For consider your calling, brothers: not many of you were wise according to worldly standards, not many were powerful, not many were of noble birth. But God chose what is foolish in the world to shame the wise; God chose what is weak in the world to shame the strong; God chose what is low and despised in the world, even things that are not, to bring to nothing things that are, so that no human being might boast in the presence of God. And because of him you are in Christ Jesus, who became to us wisdom from God, righteousness and sanctification and redemption, so that, as it is written, "Let the one who boasts, boast in the Lord." (1 Corinthians 1:22–31)

Here, Paul clearly names Jesus as Wisdom from God. Jesus *is* the Wisdom of Yahweh, and He gives us the Wisdom of Yahweh, which is to say He gives us Himself. Paul touches on this again in his Letter to the Colossians when he says,

110

> For I want you to know how great a struggle I have for you and
> for those at Laodicea and for all who have not seen me face to
> face, that their hearts may be encouraged, being knit together
> in love, to reach all the riches of full assurance of understanding
> and the knowledge of God's mystery, which is Christ, in whom
> are hidden all the treasures of wisdom and knowledge. I say this
> in order that no one may delude you with plausible arguments.
> (Colossians 2:1–4)

Here Paul states that all the treasures of wisdom are hidden in Christ, who is Wisdom.

Taking this a step further, as we have noted that Proverbs 8 and Proverbs 31 are both pictures of Wisdom, it becomes clear that Proverbs 31 is both literally about a model woman who fears the Lord and figuratively about who Christ is and His righteousness. Analogically and in actuality, the woman of Proverbs 31 embodies what the life of Christ is.[44]

Much like many Old Testament prophecies that had both immediate and later fulfillment, this passage can be understood in two different ways. It *is* a picture of the woman who fears the LORD. This woman is exemplified by Ruth the Moabite, who lives out the same kind of care and faithfulness that is praised in Proverbs 31:10–31. As we've established, in its connection to Proverbs 8, Proverbs 31:10–31 is also a description of Wisdom and therefore a description of Jesus Christ. The woman of Proverbs 31 is a personification of Wisdom, and Jesus is Wisdom Incarnate: He never rests from His labors day or night; He clothes His people both physically with clothing and spiritually with righteousness; He feeds His family, the Church, both their daily bread and His own body and blood in the Holy Supper; He speaks wisely and rightly and all of His Words are life for the hearers; He cares for the poor and the needy. Jesus is called blessed by His family, the Church, because of His sacrifice; His people are accepted and honored in the gates (they are accepted and honored by God the Father); and His works—all of creation and the Church—praise Him in the gates of the

---

44 Please note that this does not mean that Jesus is female. These two chapters, as discussed before, are spoken of in a feminine format because the abstract noun for "wisdom" in the Hebrew is in the feminine conjugation. Jesus Christ, the God-man, is male.

Lord's House. Notice how many of these deeds are similar to or aspects of the deeds Jesus Himself lists concerning John's question in Matthew 11 about whether or not He is the Christ. In Him is life, just as in Lady Wisdom there is life. As Jesus Himself points out to John, in Him "the dead are raised up" (Matthew 11:5).

TYING IT ALL TOGETHER

Now that we have seen how all of these intersect both linguistically and with regard to their subject matter, questions remain: Why is this important? What more can we glean from these connections concerning Ruth and concerning us? How does making these connections help us to better interpret both Ruth and Proverbs 31:10–31? How can this answer those feelings of inadequacy or guilt that a Law-based reading of Proverbs and Ruth might create? How does this add to the beauty of this passage as it is meant to be understood? How does it enrich our reading of these treasured passages?

RUTH

The fact that Ruth and the woman of Proverbs 31 are the same directs us to a few truths about Ruth. First of all, Ruth is truly a worthy woman. She is to be understood and admired as a woman who fears the Lord and should be honored and upheld as a good example for women. More than this, though, her status as a worthy woman and as a woman who fears the Lord, along with the fact that she is identified with this passage concerning the ideal wife, means that she is to be highly esteemed alongside other highly esteemed women in Israel's history: Sarah, Rebekah, and Leah. Here again, Ruth is being connected to the matriarchs in that she is honored and esteemed by the narrator in the same way in which they are honored and esteemed by the Israelites. It is through these matriarchs that the line of the promised Seed has continued. Eve to Sarah, Sarah to Rebekah, and Rebekah to Leah; each gives birth to a child in the lineage of the Christ. To connect Ruth with them is to indicate that she, too, is an important link in the chain leading to the promised Seed.

Understanding Ruth as worthy and as the woman who fulfills this passage in its immediate sense is also striking because of Ruth's background. Ruth is a Moabite and was a pagan and should not be a faithful servant of Yahweh; she should not be a loving and faithful daughter-in-law to Naomi. Her service to and sacrifice for Naomi is unexpected. The fact that Ruth, part of a people group often chastised and warned against in other Old Testament writings, is seen as the woman who exemplifies "the fear of the LORD" is a bold statement by the narrator. Pagans—"others"—can and do have faith in Yahweh, the one true God. They can be brought into the fold of God's chosen people. They can even be seen as the fulfillment of this passage of Proverbs. By making this point about Ruth, the narrator is also touching on one of the purposes for the Book of Ruth that we discussed in chapter 1: to show that David was right to allow believing foreigners to enter the assembly. By connecting Ruth to the woman of Proverbs 31 and showing that she is as faithful and worthy as this ideal woman, the narrator makes a solid case that Ruth belongs among God's chosen people despite her ethnic background. This individualized history of a woman who confesses Yahweh when all odds say she should not becomes an example of why David was right to allow all believing foreigners to worship Yahweh in the assembly. No one will argue with Ruth's worthiness now. The original hearers should be feeling quite sympathetic toward her by the end of the story, so their sympathy will logically extend to others like her.

PROVERBS 31:10–31, RUTH, AND US

Both the Book of Ruth and Proverbs 31:10–31 are often hijacked into "how-tos" or "you shoulds" by well-meaning interpreters (or maybe they're not so well meaning!). This is how a woman is good and pleasing to God, so go and do it. Be like Ruth. Be the woman of Proverbs 31! Never stop. Don't complain. Get busy! Here's your list of things to do to be a "good Christian woman." When we look at Ruth and the sacrifices she makes, when we read the lists of things the woman of Proverbs 31 does, it all seems quite impossible. No one can ever be that good. No one can ever be that loving and faithful, that accomplished. I haven't done this. I can't do this. Worst of all, I don't want to do this. Read on their own, interpreted in this way, both Ruth and Proverbs 31 become Law. They prescribe and they accuse.

Prescriptive texts outline what a person must or should do. (The Ten Commandments are prescriptive.) Descriptive texts describe an event, action, or person in the history of God's people and of God's work in the world. They may also reveal certain truths about humanity and God, but they are not necessarily prescriptive. This means that a descriptive text is not one that needs to be exactly imitated or followed by us, but rather one that offers certain truths or insights that we are to gain. A good example of this is the story of Jacob stealing Esau's birthright. While in the end God uses it to forward His plan for Jacob's life and lineage, it is not a prescription for us to take what we think is rightly ours by deceit (even when we believe that it is part of God's plan for us to have it). Jacob's story is not about how we should act or imitate Him, but about how God uses Jacob to create His chosen people despite Jacob's flaws and how the Lord brings about the birth of His Son. Another example might be the fact that John the Baptist did not drink wine. This, again, is descriptive of John, who had a special calling and was in a special and particular circumstance. It is not a prescription for us to always avoid alcohol. Interpreting descriptive texts as if they are prescriptive causes havoc with the pure Word of God, usually on the side of Law. This often ends up creating a works-righteousness system.

We are sinful at times; and we are baptized. Wholly holy in Baptism, the Spirit leads us, yet the old man (though drowned) rises up against the new. In the wretchedness of the old man we do not do good; of that, we need to repent. Christians do want to try, but we realize the hopelessness of trying to do it all and be it all. These are impossible tasks taken altogether. So how do we view this passage in Proverbs; how do we understand what Ruth might be teaching us?

This is where Proverbs 8 comes in to rescue us. Or rather, this is where Christ, the Wisdom from on high, comes in to rescue us. Yes, Proverbs 31:10–31 is a picture of a woman who fears the Lord. Yes, Ruth is a wonderful example for us to follow. Yes, these are standards we should live up to in regards to serving and loving our family and fearing the Lord. Yes, it seems impossible to be that good. Many may say we must strive to be like Ruth and the wise woman of Proverbs 31. However, Proverbs 31 and Ruth do not leave us striving. When put together with Proverbs 8, Proverbs 31 and Ruth become not prescriptions for everything that a woman must do and be, but a picture of who the woman who fears the Lord *is* already. When we see that Proverbs 31 and Proverbs 8 are really about Christ, we see that He has done and does do all these things for us. (Remember His own list of deeds from Matthew 11?) He has feared the Lord perfectly, He has cared for His family (that's us!), He has sacrificed Himself for others, and He never rests from His labors. Not only is Christ continuously doing all this and more *for you*, but He also does all this and more *in and through you*. This means that, ultimately, you—the mommy on the run, the wife, the single woman, the career woman, the college student, the woman searching for who she is—you already are the woman who fears the Lord by virtue of your Baptism into Christ's death and His living in and through you. You can confess with Paul: "I have been crucified with Christ. It is no longer I who live, but Christ who lives in me. And the life I now live in the flesh I live by faith in the Son of God, who loved me and gave Himself for me" (Galatians 2:20). When seen in this light, Ruth is no longer just a good example of a godly woman, but a clear type of Christ, who points us not to ourselves and our striving to be "good Christian women," but to the coming Christ, who dies for us, rises for us, creates in us the faith that clings to Him, and works to serve our neighbors through us. So the next time someone tells you how to "be a good Christian woman" by following certain steps laid out by Ruth, you can say, "Thanks, but Ruth is a picture of my Savior and Lord Jesus Christ, and He does all things well in and through me. In Him I already am just like Ruth." The next time Proverbs 31:10–31 is read on Mother's Day or confronts you at some other time, you can listen to it being read, smile, and say, "That's me."

Discussion Questions:

1. How do we find a connection between Ruth and Proverbs 31:10–31? List some of the clues given to us by the texts, the narrator, and the compilers of the Hebrew canon.

2. What are some of the linguistic and subject similarities between Proverbs 8 and Proverbs 31 discussed in this chapter?

3. Discuss the difference between a prescriptive text and a descriptive text. How is Proverbs 31 often treated—as prescriptive or as descriptive? How should it be understood?

4. Similarly, is Ruth sometimes treated as a prescription for how we should act? How does our perception of Ruth and of how Ruth speaks to us today change if we understand her and her history as descriptive?

5. How do the New Testament passages discussed in this chapter help us as we interpret these two chapters of Proverbs and Ruth?

CHAPTER 6

RUTH 4:1–17: REDEMPTION

OPENING PRAYER: HEAVENLY FATHER, You are our Kinsman-Redeemer; continue to redeem us from those things that enslave us—sin, death, and the world—so that we may serve You in Your kingdom; through Jesus Christ, Your Son, our Lord, who lives and reigns with You and the Holy Spirit, one God, now and forever. Amen.

Introduction

IN THE PREVIOUS CHAPTER OF THIS BOOK, we discussed Ruth's connection to Proverbs 31:10–31 and Proverbs 8. Through the exploration of those two texts, and through our study of the Book of Ruth so far, we have seen clearly how Ruth the person is a type of Christ. She serves Naomi, is faithful to Yahweh, sacrifices her own well-being, and observes the spirit, not just the letter, of the Law. In chapter 4 of the Book of Ruth, the action shifts to Boaz, and the narrator offers a summary of events that happen further down the road.

So far, the Book of Ruth has focused on a short period of time and, in large part, on the actions of the women, Ruth and Naomi. With the shift in focus to Boaz, we find more parallels with Christ. Then, as the narrator takes us forward in time, he reveals how the Book of Ruth connects to David and beyond. The narrative portion of the Book of Ruth ends with verse 17. The final verses, the genealogy, will be explored in the next chapter of this book.

Verse By Verse Analysis
READ RUTH 4:1–12

Ruth chapter 3 left us with Ruth and Naomi waiting for Boaz to "settle the matter" (Ruth 3:18). Naomi is confident that Boaz will do so that same day, and the narrator shows in chapter 4 that she is right to have such confidence. The tense in 4:1 ("Now Boaz had . . . ") suggests that even while they are discussing this, Boaz is busy making the arrangements. As touched on in the discussion of the two passages from Proverbs, "the gates" played an important role in Israelite culture. They were a place of meeting where transactions and legal issues could be attended to properly and witnessed by a trusted group of town elders. Boaz immediately makes his way to the gate in order to properly attend to the legal issues of redeeming Naomi's plot of land.

The phrase "and behold" occurs here as it did in the beginning of Ruth chapter 2. Again, this is the narrator drawing our attention to something important. He is implying that, like Ruth happening upon Boaz's field, it is no coincidence that the nearer redeemer comes by. First of all, Boaz probably knew that the man would be coming in from the threshing floor that morning, just as he had left the threshing floor to come into the city. Second, Yahweh is still at work behind the scenes, so the narrator again implies that more than just human agency has caused the right man to come along at the right time. Yahweh Himself is making sure that all goes well for the redemption of Naomi's land.

In the ESV, Boaz calls the nearer redeemer "friend." However, this translation is not really faithful to the original text. The Hebrew is actually more like "so-and-so or a certain one." There is no sense of friend or friendship here; the term is more neutral. We should note too that the nearer redeemer is not named. By omitting his name, the narrator gives us a clue as to the outcome. As stated earlier, Hebrew names often have meaning and can tell us something about the person. When a person is unnamed, it means he is not important and is perhaps even somewhat dishonorable. This should suggest to us that the nearer redeemer will probably refuse the right of redemption. If he is not important enough to be named, then he will not do much to help Ruth and Naomi.

Once Boaz has made sure to secure the nearer redeemer's presence, he gathers ten of the elders. The verb *took* probably indicates that he actively sought them out and brought them together. It is not a passive verb, as though Boaz merely waited for people to come by the gate. He was active in carrying out his promise to Ruth to settle the matters of the redemption and her proposal of marriage quickly. Ten men are chosen because ten is the number of completeness. It means that everything was complete and in proper order for a transaction to take place.

Boaz then explains the situation, telling the nearer redeemer that Naomi is selling the plot of land that belonged to her husband, Elimelech. What Elimelech had probably done when he left Judah was sell the grain the land would yield (its usufruct, or right to plant and harvest from it) and not the land itself. The land then could be returned to the owner at the Year of Jubilee, in accordance with God's command. However, the Year of Jubilee was probably some years away and could not be of help to Ruth and Naomi in their immediate needs. Therefore, since she no longer has sons who can do so, Naomi is transferring the right of redemption to a male relative who is able to redeem it. An Israelite woman did not usually own land herself, since she was under the protection of her closest male relative (husband, father, son, brother, even grandson), but there seems to be a stipulation allowing her to hold the land until, for instance, the son came of age to inherit it.[45] This allowed for the widow to be protected and provided for until a male relative could help her. See, for example, Numbers 27:5–11:

> Here the daughters of the deceased man Zelophehad come to Moses for help when their father dies. They have no means of sustenance, because they have no inheritance and they have no husbands or brothers to care for them. Their father's possessions were to be distributed among his brothers (their uncles). So the Lord commands that there be a provision to protect daughters without a close male relative to inherit their father's property. It is possible that similar care is given to widows.

The principle of the widow being able to hold the right to redemption until a son came of age seems to be referenced in 2 Kings 8:1–6:

> "Now Elisha had said to the woman whose son he had restored to life, "Arise, and depart with your household, and sojourn

---

45   Wilch, 328.

wherever you can, for the LORD has called for a famine, and it will come upon the land for seven years." So the woman arose and did according to the word of the man of God. She went with her household and sojourned in the land of the Philistines seven years. And at the end of the seven years, when the woman returned from the land of the Philistines, she went to appeal to the king for her house and her land. Now the king was talking with Gehazi the servant of the man of God, saying, "Tell me all the great things that Elisha has done." And while he was telling the king how Elisha had restored the dead to life, behold, the woman whose son he had restored to life appealed to the king for her house and her land. And Gehazi said, "My lord, O king, here is the woman, and here is her son whom Elisha restored to life." And when the king asked the woman, she told him. So the king appointed an official for her, saying, "Restore all that was hers, together with all the produce of the fields from the day that she left the land until now."

These two instances show that it was possible for a woman to be cared for by allowing her to have charge of her husband's land or her father's inheritance when there was no other close male relative to provide for her. In the case of the widow whom Elisha helped, her son would eventually inherit the land. Until then, the king considers it "her" land. Naomi is also left without any close male relatives. So the people probably see the land as hers until she dies or until a close male relative was able to help her. The problem for Naomi is that its usufruct has been sold and she cannot lay claim to it at present.

It is advantageous to Naomi to transfer the right of redemption, because she cannot afford to redeem the land's usufruct for herself and therefore cannot live off of it until the Year of Jubilee—and because the one who redeems it also has an obligation to care for Naomi as a widow. Exodus 22:22 reads: "You shall not mistreat any widow or fatherless child." To redeem the land without properly caring for the widow would be to mistreat her, and it would go against the very nature and purpose of the kinsman-redeemer provision, which is to restore the land to the rightful owner or care for his family.

Furthermore, it is Naomi who is selling the land and not Ruth, although Ruth's husband, Mahlon, would have been Elimelech's heir. This is because, if there was no male heir, only a female Israelite could inherit the land; she was then required to marry within her clan:

> And Moses commanded the people of Israel according to the word of the LORD, saying, "The tribe of the people of Joseph is right. This is what the LORD commands concerning the daughters of Zelophehad, 'Let them marry whom they think best, only they shall marry within the clan of the tribe of their father. The inheritance of the people of Israel shall not be transferred from one tribe to another, for every one of the people of Israel shall hold on to the inheritance of the tribe of his fathers. And every daughter who possesses an inheritance in any tribe of the people of Israel shall be wife to one of the clan of the tribe of her father, so that every one of the people of Israel may possess the inheritance of his fathers. So no inheritance shall be transferred from one tribe to another, for each of the tribes of the people of Israel shall hold on to its own inheritance.'" (Numbers 36:5–9)

The same principle likely applies here. Naomi is an Israelite, so she can hold the inheritance, but Ruth is not, and as a foreign wife has either little or no entitlement to the inheritance.

In the following verses, it is best to understand the word *buy* as "acquire" (it is translated this way in verse 5). Verse 4 would then read, "Acquire it in the presence of those sitting here and in the presence of the elders of my people." Money would not necessarily have changed hands at this occasion, because whoever redeemed it would have to buy it from the person who had bought the usufruct from Elimelech.

What Boaz and the nearer redeemer are doing here is merely deciding who will act on the right of redemption. At first, the nearer redeemer agrees to acquire the right to redemption. The nearer redeemer would gain all of the profit from the land, and the only obligation would be to care for Naomi until her death. (He had no obligation to care for Ruth, as she was a foreign widow.[46]) Also, without an heir from Elimelech's family, the nearer redeemer would be able to add the land to his own property and pass it along as inheritance to his children.

---

46   Wilch, 330.

There would certainly be no self-sacrifice involved on the part of the nearer redeemer according to this scenario. This would have been a good deal for him.

Levirate Marriage: We discussed Levirate marriage briefly in chapter 1. To review and expand, Levirate marriage is the provision in the law where the brother of a man who dies childless would take his brother's wife and help her to conceive an heir for his brother. This allowed the deceased man's land to remain in his family. The child begotten by the brother and the widow would be considered both the legal child of the deceased and the legal child of the brother. Deuteronomy 25:5–10 offers instructions concerning Levirate marriage directly from the mouth of Yahweh:

If brothers dwell together, and one of them dies and has no son, the wife of the dead man shall not be married outside the family to a stranger. Her husband's brother shall go in to her and take her as his wife and perform the duty of a husband's brother to her. And the first son whom she bears shall succeed to the name of his dead brother, that his name may not be blotted out of Israel. And if the man does not wish to take his brother's wife, then his brother's wife shall go up to the gate to the elders and say, 'My husband's brother refuses to perpetuate his brother's name in Israel; he will not perform the duty of a husband's brother to me.' Then the elders of his city shall call him and speak to him, and if he persists, saying 'I do not wish to take her,' then his brother's wife shall go up to him in the presence of the elders and pull his sandal off his foot and spit in his face. And she shall answer and say, 'So shall it be done to the man who does not build up his brother's house.' And the name of his house shall be called in Israel, 'The house of him who had his sandal pulled off.'

Although the entire law is spelled out here, it was in practice before the Mosaic Law was given (see Judah and Tamar in Genesis 38). It seems there was a long-standing custom of Levirate marriage that was codified (or at the very least expressly dictated) by Yahweh once He gave Moses the Law on Mount Sinai. The law does several things:

1. It provides for the widow to be cared for first by her brother-in-law and then by the son begotten by them;

2. It provides an heir to continue the name of the deceased;

3. It also provides the heir to maintain the land and its inheritance;

4. It offers further protection for the widow by giving her several means of recourse should the brother-in-law refuse Levirate marriage; and

5. It provides a means of dishonoring the brother who will not abide by the law for Levirate marriage.

However, Boaz bursts this little bubble when he says in verse 5 that when the nearer redeemer acquires the land, he also acquires Ruth. The translation here in the ESV and in most other versions is "you will acquire Ruth," but Wilch argues that the verb is actually "I will acquire Ruth," meaning that Boaz would marry her.[47] This makes sense, because the right of redemption did not mean that the nearer redeemer was obligated to marry Ruth; he could have refused Ruth's hand while buying the land.

Levirate marriage—wherein the brother of the deceased marries his widow to produce a male heir—is not part and parcel of the redemption process. There is no indication that this man is a brother of Elimelech. He may be a cousin, meaning that he had no obligation to fulfill the separate duty of Levirate marriage. Additionally, the real complication here is that if Boaz marries Ruth and produces an heir, then the heir (begotten in the names of Mahlon and Elimelech), and not the nearer redeemer's children, inherits the land. Nor would the nearer redeemer be able to keep the produce of the land; it would go to the heir. Ultimately, the nearer redeemer would pay for a plot of land from which he would earn no income. This would indeed threaten to ruin his inheritance. John R. Wilch makes a convincing argument for this change based on grammar and textual criticism as well (looking at textual variants between copies we have of the Old Testament and finding the most likely reading).[48]

The nearer redeemer's response also fits better with Wilch's reading of "I acquire Ruth" rather than "you acquire Ruth." If Boaz were saying that the man must marry Ruth, he would not have much support from either Law or custom. And even if the man did feel obligated to marry Ruth, he would not necessarily have to conceive a child with her. After marrying her or taking her into his household, he could avoid performing the duty of Levirate marriage and thereby protect his new inheritance. The threat here is that in acquiring Ruth, Boaz's clear intention is to produce an heir, which would eliminate the nearer

---

47 Wilch, 312–13.

48 Ibid., 312–13 and 330–32.

redeemer's gain from the land. Therefore, the nearer redeemer offers the right of redemption back to Boaz using a custom so outdated by the time of David that the narrator has to explain it: the nearer redeemer removes his sandal and gives it to Boaz to make the contract legal and binding.

The narrator here explains a former custom, but he also builds suspense by breaking off the dialogue where he does. The hearer or reader waits, anxious to know how this will all turn out. It has been quite the whirlwind in the Book of Ruth.

- First, there is the dramatic setting of famine, death, and loss;
- then the anticipation caused by the unfinished betrothal type-scene;
- next there are the heightened stakes of Ruth's nighttime visit to Boaz;
- then there is the narrator's surprise revelation of the nearer redeemer;
- then the anticipation of the town meeting;
- and, finally, the seemingly lost chance for Ruth and Boaz's marriage when the nearer redeemer consents to buy the field.

The drama continues to build, and the reader/hearer is still on the edge of her seat. And now Boaz throws out this statement and threat, and the narrator pauses to explain a custom. It seems so out of place! He is building our suspense with the decision of old "so-and-so."

The nearer redeemer decides that, on second thought, he would rather maintain his current way of life than take a chance on redeeming the field only to have Boaz and Ruth produce an heir. Against this backdrop of the nearer redeemer's clear selfishness, Boaz announces in very clear, legal terms what he is doing. By speaking the words, the deed is accomplished. Boaz calls on the elders and the rest of the people at the gate (there were other members of the community present as well) to witness to the fact that he has bought the right to redemption from Naomi and that he has acquired Ruth. He clearly states that he will take her as his wife for the purpose of producing an heir in order to preserve the name of the dead. He closes by reminding them that they are witnesses. The people agree to be witnesses for Boaz; this is important because the transaction was not recorded in writing, so the testimony of the elders and other men at the gate serves as the legal contract and can be called upon for clarification in the case of a dispute.

They then do something that may seem odd to us in the midst of a legal procedure, but it is very much a part of the fabric of the Book of Ruth. They pronounce a blessing on Boaz and Ruth. First, they ask that Yahweh make Ruth like Rachel and Leah, who built up the house of Israel (interestingly enough, Rachel is buried near Bethlehem; see Genesis 35:16–20). Here again, and more explicitly now, Ruth's life is tied to that of the matriarchs. This is striking, again because Ruth is a foreigner and because Rachel and Leah are the mothers of the sons who became the twelve tribes of Israel. (Included in addition to the twelve are Joseph's sons Ephraim and Manasseh, who are considered half-tribes). Genesis 35:22c–26 lists their sons, from whom the twelve tribes of Israel were created:

> Now the sons of Jacob were twelve. The sons of Leah: Reuben (Jacob's firstborn), Simeon, Levi, Judah, Issachar, and Zebulun. The sons of Rachel: Joseph and Benjamin. The sons of Bilhah, Rachel's servant: Dan and Naphtali. The sons of Zilpah, Leah's servant: Gad and Asher. These were the sons of Jacob who were born to him in Paddan-aram.

By asking this blessing on Ruth and Boaz, the townspeople are showing what high honor is due to Boaz for his willingness to voluntarily redeem the land and marry Ruth in order to produce an heir for Mahlon and Elimelech. Without the sons of Jacob, Rachel, and Leah, there would be no Israel. They are literally the ones through whom God created His own people, the Israelites. To ask that Yahweh make Ruth like Rachel and Leah is a significant blessing; it is asking that she and her offspring become as important to Israel as those who first built up Israel. Just as without Rachel and Leah there would be no Israel, is there a way that without Ruth there is no Israel? This blessing asks that Ruth be as important to the history and life of Israel as Rachel and Leah!

To build up a house is a common expression in the Old Testament that means "to bear children and enrich the household of the husband or patriarch." It is often the desire of the women of Genesis who are barren that they might bear children and thereby "build up" their husband's house. This would have been especially true of bearing sons, because it is through sons that names are handed down and inheritances are given from generation to generation. In his commentary on Genesis, Luther says:

> Thus this expression is common in Scripture, that the wife is called
> a household building because she bears and brings up the offspring.
> . . . Let us, therefore, obey the Word of God and recognize our wives
> as a building of God. Not only is the house built through them by
> procreation and other services that are necessary in a household;
> but the husbands themselves are built through them, because wives
> are, as it were, a nest and a dwelling place where husbands can go to
> spend their time and dwell with joy.[49]

When Luther puts it this way, we see that the request that Ruth build up Boaz's house is a request not just for children, but also for comfort and happiness for them both.

In the next portion of the blessing, the people ask that Boaz's name be renowned in Bethlehem and that he act worthily in Ephrathah. This is already somewhat fulfilled in that Boaz has already been called worthy and is at that moment acting worthily. Additionally, their blessing of Boaz in the gates, among all the elders of the town, already begins to fulfill the blessing that his name be renowned. They then ask a blessing that the house of Boaz be like that of Perez. Perez was the son of Judah and Tamar (see the callout), and Perez's descendants became the dominant clan in the tribe of Judah.[50]

---

49   Martin Luther, Luther's Works, American Edition, vol. 1, *Lectures on Genesis: Chapters 1–5*, Ed. Jaroslav Pelikan. (St. Louis: Concordia Publishing House, 1960), 132-134.

50   See Wilch, 349.

{ *Tamar and Judah* }

The story of Tamar and Judah in Genesis 38 has interesting parallels to the Ruth story in that it also involves the practice of Levirate marriage, but it involves people much less worthy than Ruth or Boaz. Tamar was Judah's daughter-in-law. Her husband, Judah's son Er, was wicked, and Yahweh put him to death (v. 7). He died without leaving an heir, so Judah had his second son, Onan, go to Tamar to perform the Levir duty (v. 8). Onan refused, and so God also put him to death. Therefore, Judah promised Tamar his third son when that son was grown, but did not follow through on the promise, fearing that the third son would also die. Tamar then tricked Judah so she would conceive by him. The resulting children were Perez and his twin, Zerah. Perez showed his cunning and strength even as a baby by getting around his brother, Zerah, to be the firstborn, even though Zerah's hand came out first.

We should pay some special attention to the word *offspring* in verse 12. It is an important word in Scripture and should be noted especially as it connects this portion of the Book of Ruth to the Book of Genesis. The Hebrew word for offspring can also be translated as "seed." The following verses also use this special word:

Genesis 3:15: "[Yahweh said,] 'I will put enmity between you and the woman, and between your offspring and her offspring; He shall bruise your head, and you shall bruise His heel.'"

Genesis 13:14–16: "The LORD said to Abram, after Lot had separated from him, 'Lift up your eyes and look from the place where you are, northward and southward and eastward and westward, for all the land that you see I will give to you and to your offspring forever. I will make your offspring as the dust of the earth, so that if one can count the dust of the earth, your offspring also can be counted.'"

Genesis 15:4–5: (Yahweh speaking to Abraham): "And behold, the word of the LORD came to him: 'This man shall not be your heir; your very own son shall be your heir.' And He brought him outside and said, 'Look toward heaven, and number the stars, if you are able to number them.' Then He said to him, 'So shall your offspring be.'"

Genesis 22:15–18: (during the narrative of the sacrifice of Isaac): "And the angel of the LORD called to Abraham a second time from heaven and said, 'By Myself I have sworn, declares the LORD, because you have done this and have not withheld your son, your only son, I will surely bless you, and I will surely multiply your offspring as the stars of heaven and as the sand that is on the seashore. And your offspring shall possess the gate of his enemies, and in your offspring shall all the nations of the earth be blessed, because you have obeyed My voice.'"

The blessing for Boaz's offspring should remind the hearers and readers of God's promise for the offspring, or seed, of Eve and of Abraham. Through their seed, all the nations were to be blessed. Using the same word here ties the story of Ruth and Boaz to the greater story of God's work through the matriarchs, the patriarchs, and even Adam and Eve.

As this section closes, you may have noticed in your reading that a *leitwort* extends from the previous chapter into this one. The *leitwort* is *redeem*. It is used most often in this section in reference to the land; the transaction is for the redemption of the land. Again, though, this word does not refer only to the immediate proceedings. By emphasizing it, it's clear that the narrator wants us to think about spiritual redemption as well. The word *redeem* means to "buy back." Here Boaz buys back the land for Naomi and Ruth. Yahweh also works to buy back His people. Since the land was a precursor of sorts for the eternal inheritance God had in store for the Israelites, to buy back this earthly inheritance also restores them to their rightful place in God's kingdom and in eternal life.

Until now, the narrative has covered a short period of probably a few months in the lives of Ruth, Naomi, and Boaz. We know this because it begins just before the harvest and ends when they were threshing the wheat and barley. In these last few verses, however, the narrator quickly covers a span of about a year's time. The narrator moves immediately from the transaction and blessing to Boaz taking Ruth as his wife and going to her so that she would conceive. This pace shows the reader just how true and faithful Boaz was to his word and promise. Just as Boaz quickly settled the matter of the right of redemption the morning after Ruth's request, so too he settles the matter of this above-and-beyond Levirate marriage quickly and faithfully.

The narrator is also deliberate in his use of Yahweh's name in the next clause. Throughout most of Ruth, Yahweh is referred to mostly in prayers and blessings. But here and in a few phrases early in the Book of Ruth, references to Yahweh are different in that they speak about His activity. The first is when the narrator notes that Naomi is returning because she had heard that "[Yahweh] had visited His people and given them food" (1:6). Here the narrator draws attention to Yahweh's gracious works. Naomi also says that Yahweh's hand has gone against her, speaking directly to Yahweh's activity in His hiddenness. Beyond those instances in the first chapter, the rest of the references to Yahweh are blessings in His name or petitions to Him—until this moment in chapter 4. Here, the narrator clearly points to Yahweh as the one who gives Ruth conception. This phrase or a similar one occurs in many other important passages in the Old Testament, as well:

Genesis 21:1–2: "The LORD visited Sarah as He had said, and the LORD did to Sarah as He had promised. And Sarah conceived and bore Abraham a son in his old age at the time of which God had spoken to him."

Genesis 25:21: "And Isaac prayed to the LORD for his wife, because she was barren. And the LORD granted his prayer, and Rebekah his wife conceived."

Genesis 29:31–32: "When the LORD saw that Leah was hated, He opened her womb, but Rachel was barren. And Leah conceived and bore a son, and she called his name Reuben, for she said, 'Because the LORD has looked upon my affliction; for now my husband will love me.'"

Genesis 30:22–23: Then God remembered Rachel, and God listened to her and opened her womb. She conceived and bore a son and said, "God has taken away my reproach."

Sarah, Rebekah, Leah, and Rachel each is given a scene in which Yahweh gives her conception and she then bears a son. Again, the narrator is drawing a connection between Ruth and the matriarchs of Israel.

{ *Conception and Infertility* }

God is the giver of all life, and conception and children are gifts from His hand. However, many among us suffer from infertility, miscarriage, and loss through stillbirth. For these couples, the fact that Yahweh gives conception can be a painful truth. If Yahweh gives conception, why has He not given it to me? What have I done to cause Him to withhold children from me? Is there something I should do differently to make God favorable toward me so He will give me children? We do not always know why we struggle with infertility, sadness, illnesses, and other difficulties. These conditions are a part of a fallen, broken world and are not necessarily a sign that we are being punished for a specific sin. What we do know is that Yahweh worked through the specific gift of conception for specific women (Sarah, Leah, and Mary, for instance), in order to save us "through child-bearing," that is, through the birth of Jesus (1 Timothy 2:15).

Rather than try to look into the mystery of God's ways, we look to how He has revealed Himself to us in Jesus. In the meantime, God is with those who struggle in their sadness and sorrow, strengthening them through His Word and Sacraments, and pointing them to the fact that Jesus is here for them. When Christ came as a baby, born of a virgin, He won the victory over the brokenness of this world, and when He comes again, that victory will be fully seen. He will heal and restore all things, including infertility.

In Ruth 4:14, the women praise Yahweh on behalf of Naomi because He had not left Naomi without a redeemer. Notice how this brings us full circle: "And both Mahlon and Chilion died, so that the woman was left without her two sons and her husband" (Ruth 1:5). Naomi's beginning state is one of having been left; she even feels that Yahweh has left her. Yet here the narrator is showing us that, indeed, Naomi has not been left. The Lord has provided a redeemer. Again, the women pray that the name of the redeemer, in this case the baby, Obed, be renowned in Israel. They say that the baby will be a restorer of life and a nourisher to her in her old age. Through Obed, Elimelech's family is "resurrected" from namelessness and loss of inheritance. He will "perpetuate the name of the dead in his inheritance," just as Boaz had vowed (4:5).

The women praise Ruth as "better than seven sons." This was a high compliment, indeed. Sons were a precious gift, because they carried on the family name and inheritance. Seven refers to a complete number, the perfect amount, and seven sons is "the ideal number of sons for a family."[51] Job had seven sons who died and then seven sons to replace them. Interestingly, Jesse had eight sons, David being the eighth and, of course, the greatest.[52] Ruth is one better, in a sense, than seven sons. She has done more for Naomi in her demonstrations of *chesed* than seven sons.

In the next verse, verse 16, Naomi takes "the child" on her lap and becomes his nurse, or guardian. In chapter 1 of this book, we noted that the word used of Mahlon and Chilion was the word for "young sons" and not the word that would be used of adult sons. We also said that the word was used again in chapter 4, verse 16 and formed an inclusio. Here we come to the capping moment of that inclusio. Everything that has happened between chapter 1 verse 5 and chapter 4 verse 16 has led to this moment. Ruth's confession, their journey, the harvest, Ruth's work in the harvest, Boaz's generosity, Ruth's risk, Boaz arranging the redemption, Ruth and Boaz's marriage, and the birth of the baby have all been in service of this moment when the "child" (the same word as in Ruth 1:5) is laid in Naomi's lap, finally filling the emptiness left by the deaths of her husband and her sons. Yahweh was at work the whole time to bring life from death, fullness from emptiness, pleasantness from bitterness (see Ruth 1:19–20).

In acknowledgement of the greatness of this event, the women of the neighborhood name the child. Usually, the child would be named

---

51   Wilch, 369.

52   Jesse had eight sons, David being the eighth who surpassed the biblical and cultural ideal of seven sons. Only seven of Jesse's sons pass before Samuel in the field, and then when none of them are suitable, David is called. David is the eighth son to pass before Samuel and the eighth and youngest son of Jesse (1 Samuel 16:1–11). 1 Samuel 17:12 also states that Jesse had eight sons, while only seven are listed later in 1 Chronicles 2:13–15. John R. Wilch notes that another scholar suggests that one of the sons could have died before he had produced an heir and thus been left out of the list in 1 Chronicles (see Wilch, 379, n. 93). That David is the eighth son shows that he is an exceptional and surpasses the ideal. David was especially chosen by God and had a unique place in His plan.

by his father. Here, though, the same women who welcomed Naomi home from Moab name the child. They call him Naomi's son, because he replaces Naomi's dead children as the heir of Elimelech. Since Naomi can no longer give birth to a child herself, Ruth has done so on her behalf. The women name the child *Obed*, which means servant. He will serve Naomi by now acting as her redeemer. Now that Naomi has a grandson, she has a nearest kinsman. The inheritance will pass into his name and his hands when he grows, and he will be able to sustain and care for them both. *Obed* also means "worshiper," which points to the idea that Obed will be a faithful follower and worshiper of Yahweh, just as Boaz and Ruth are.

In this communal naming of Obed (Ruth 4:17), there are two words in common with verses 11 and 14 of chapter 4. These are the words *renowned* and *name*. In verse 11, they blessed Boaz, asking that he be renowned; and in verse 14, they bless Naomi and the child by asking that his name be renowned in Israel.

When the women name Obed in 4:17, they already begin to fulfill both of these blessings. Obed's name is renowned already, as he is known throughout the community and named by the community. Boaz's name is renowned through his descendants. The narrator points us to this idea when he ends with the comment that Obed was the father of Jesse, who was the father of David. David, of course, was King of Israel, a renowned name indeed!

So this little story has a big ending. From Naomi the empty to Naomi the full, ancestor of a king. From Moabite Ruth the foreigner to Ruth, the faithful ancestor of a king. From Boaz the worthy to Boaz, the renowned ancestor of a king. From Obed the baby to Obed, the ancestor of a king. From Bethlehem to Jerusalem. The narrator brings us out of the microcosm of this seemingly simple story to the overarching story of David the king and the history of the kingdoms of Israel and Judah.

{ *Microcosm* }

A microcosm is a depiction of a world in a smaller format. In literature, this means that the world of the story is a miniature version of a larger world or reality. The events told about this smaller world can be applied to the larger world. By using a microcosm, the author or narrator can focus in on a subject and create sympathy and attachment to the individuals in it, while at the same time addressing themes and truths about the larger world to which the story can be analogically applied.

So here in Ruth, the smaller world is Moab to Bethlehem with Ruth, Naomi, and Boaz at the center. Their story, while true and significant in and of itself, is symbolic of the larger story of God's people. What Yahweh does for them, He also does for all of His people throughout all of time. The Scriptures add another dimension to this, though. Not only is Ruth a smaller picture of the way God typically cares for and tends to His people, Ruth's life is an actual piece of the puzzle in His overall work of redemption.

INTERPRETATION

A lot has happened in these final verses of the Book of Ruth. Many of the main themes are brought to conclusion here. In his retelling of the true story of Ruth, Naomi, and Boaz, the narrator has created a masterpiece of literature (remember: literature is not synonymous with fiction). This masterpiece is, in and of itself, worthy of attention for its skill and depth. It seems simple at first glance, but the narrator was skilled at his work. The inclusios, chiasms, word choices, structure, and subtleties of this narrative all come together in the end to point the hearer or reader to God's work for His people.

As we said at the beginning, there are many layers to the significance of this not-so-simple-after-all story.

THE NEARER REDEEMER AS FOIL

In a stroke of literary genius, the narrator depicts the nearer redeemer so that he is not really important in and of himself, but rather as a foil for Boaz. In literature, a foil character displays many opposite traits to those of a main or more important character. The foil helps emphasize the (usually better) traits of the more important or central figure in the story. The nearer redeemer serves this role in the Book of Ruth. He is a foil against which Boaz's worthy characteristics come into greater relief.

NAMES

First of all, the nearer redeemer is unnamed. As we discussed above, Boaz merely calls him "a certain one" or "so-and-so." This is not equivalent to "friend" as the ESV has it. The original Hebrew expresses a much more careless or disinterested attitude. The nearer redeemer does not merit the consideration (as he will go on to prove very quickly) afforded a real friend. Furthermore, there seems to be a slight connection between the custom of drawing off the sandal and the custom of shaming a man who refuses to be a Levir as recorded in Deuteronomy 25:10. Not only is he unnamed but, by way of association, he and his household might be thought of as "the house of he who had his sandal pulled off." In a stroke of irony, he seals his own fate in pulling off his own sandal to refuse the right of redemption. The fact that he is not named is a great contrast to the blessing asked (and fulfilled) on behalf of Boaz: that Boaz's name be renowned. Through Obed and his other descendants, and indeed, through the very writing of and hearing or reading of the Book of Ruth, Boaz's name is renowned—not renowned only in Israel but throughout all of time. The unnamed nearer redeemer, meanwhile, has gone down in history as "so-and-so" as befits his insignificance and selfishness.

GENEROSITY AND *CHESED*

The nearer redeemer's selfishness in not being willing to jeopardize his own inheritance throws into greater relief the generosity of Boaz. Redeeming Naomi's land and then marrying in order to produce an heir would have been just as costly for Boaz as for the nearer redeemer. Yet Boaz is willing to pay this cost. His generosity to Ruth and Naomi is evident throughout the narrative. He instructs Ruth to glean closer to his harvesters so she can find more grain. He instructs his harvesters to actually leave more for her to glean. He invites her to the meal for the workers and feeds her so much food that she is able to take the extra home to Naomi. Boaz also loads Ruth down with an ephah of barley at the threshing floor. His generosity has been evident all along, and the nearer redeemer's selfish nature emphasizes Boaz's generosity even more.

Boaz's generosity is also more than everyday kindness. By acquiring both Ruth and the field, he is displaying *chesed*, or faithfulness and loving-kindness. This, as we have noted, is a characteristic of Yahweh. It is more than a nice feeling or romantic love or even love of family. *Chesed* is a love that is never-ending in service to the loved one, is self-sacrificial, and is always faithful; it is the love that Yahweh has for His people. Again, here the nearer redeemer offers a stark contrast. He is unwilling to sacrifice for the good of another person. The nearer redeemer has in mind only his self-interest. His actions stem from greed and fear, and his initial commitment to redeem the land (based on having to care for Naomi for only a short time), is easily broken when he realizes the true sacrifice he would be making. He is unfaithful. The nearer redeemer's clear shortcomings highlight even more just how far above and beyond the Law Boaz goes for the sake of Naomi, Ruth, and the name of Elimelech.

BOAZ AS A TYPE OF CHRIST

In chapters 3 and 4, the type of Christ moves from Ruth to Boaz. Boaz's Christlike characteristics have been increasing since the beginning. He is first introduced to us as "a worthy man" (2:1). This is a characteristic of Jesus Christ, who is Wisdom Incarnate. Also, Boaz's generosity and kindness in chapters 2 and 3 demonstrate that he goes above and beyond the letter to the spirit of the Law. This is what Jesus does in all of His earthly life, as well as in His suffering, death, and resurrection. The *chesed* (*agape* is the Greek word for the same concept in the New Testament) shown by Boaz throughout the Book of Ruth points to Yahweh's consistent *chesed* to His people throughout the Old Testament up to this point.

Out of this *chesed*, Boaz acquires and redeems a foreign woman and the land in order to save an Israelite family from extinction. This is a picture of Yahweh's work of acquiring and redeeming. The Israelites sing of this work in relation to Yahweh's *chesed* after the exodus from Egypt:

You have led in Your steadfast love the people whom You have
> redeemed;
You have guided them by Your strength to Your holy abode.
The peoples have heard; they tremble;
> pangs have seized the inhabitants of Philistia.
Now are the chiefs of Edom dismayed;
> trembling seizes the leaders of Moab;
>> all the inhabitants of Canaan have melted away.
Terror and dread fall upon them;
> because of the greatness of Your arm, they are still as a stone,
>> till Your people, O LORD, pass by,
> till the people pass by whom You have purchased.
>>>>> (Exodus 15:13–16)

"Steadfast love" in verse 13 above is the translation for *chesed*, and "purchased" in the final verse is the same as the word for "redeem." Based on His *chesed*, God redeemed His people from Egypt. And just as God redeemed His people out of slavery to the Egyptians, which was one of the responsibilities of a kinsman-redeemer, so Boaz redeems Ruth and Naomi by buying the land, another responsibility of the kinsman-redeemer. Yahweh is Israel's kinsman-redeemer.

Yahweh is also our kinsman-redeemer because He has redeemed and acquired all Christians through the sacrifice of Jesus Christ:

> For the grace of God has appeared, bringing salvation for all people, training us to renounce ungodliness and worldly passions, and to live self-controlled, upright, and godly lives in the present age, waiting for our blessed hope, the appearing of the glory of our great God and Savior Jesus Christ, who gave Himself for us to redeem us from all lawlessness and to purify for Himself a people for His own possession who are zealous for good works. (Titus 2:11–14)

Boaz's actions in redeeming and acquiring Ruth and Elimelech's land coincide with God's actions of redemption. Like Jesus, Boaz sacrifices his own interests in order to do this work, making Boaz a type of Christ. Boaz's parallels with Christ are aptly summed up by Psalm 15:

O Lord, who shall sojourn in Your tent?
Who shall dwell on Your holy hill?
He who walks blamelessly and does what is right
and speaks truth in his heart;
who does not slander with his tongue
and does no evil to his neighbor,
nor takes up a reproach against his friend;
in whose eyes a vile person is despised,
but who honors those who fear the Lord;
who swears to his own hurt and does not change;
who does not put out his money at interest
and does not take a bribe against the innocent.
He who does these things shall never be moved.

While this psalm of David is a prophecy of Christ, many of the statements made here also remind us of David's ancestor, Boaz. Boaz honors Ruth, who fears Yahweh. He swears to help Ruth and Naomi, although he knows that doing so will hurt his income. He knows that to pay for the land and produce an heir for it means he will never recover the expense of the land, since it will all go to Naomi, Ruth, and Obed. Yet Boaz does not change his mind. He charges full force into what needs to be done. Jesus, too, knows that He must sacrifice everything, even His own life, yet He goes willingly forward to be arrested, tried, tortured, and crucified. Boaz expected nothing in return for his gifts of grain and the land; he charged no "interest." He protected the innocent, Ruth and Naomi. Jesus does all these things even more perfectly and fully than Boaz, and Jesus does them for all people in all time. Boaz's actions and characteristics point us to Jesus.

OBED, THE NEAREST REDEEMER

In verses 13–17, we are introduced to Obed. His conception is miraculous in that it is clearly given by Yahweh, as the narrator tells us. Obed's birth makes him the nearest redeemer for Naomi and Ruth. When he comes of age, it will be his responsibility to care for the land and to care for his grandmother and mother. The townspeople acknowledge this when they declare that Yahweh has not left Naomi without a redeemer. They are referring not to Boaz, but to Obed. His name, meaning "servant" or "worshiper," emphasizes that he will be faithful to Yahweh, and his name becomes renowned throughout all of Israel. Obed also, by his very existence, resurrects the line of Elimelech and Mahlon. His life is the resurrection, so to speak, of the dead, whose names will now be perpetuated in their inheritance. Finally, Obed is a baby and as a baby is acknowledged as all of these things—redeemer, servant/worshiper, and resurrector. Obed, therefore, also becomes a type of Christ, the baby whose conception was the most miraculous of all, who was sent to save the world by redeeming it with His very own blood, who served and worshiped God perfectly, and who is the resurrection and the life for all people (see John 11). This connection is a bit more remote than that of Boaz and Ruth, but there is no mistaking that it is there.

Three types of Christ in one short book—such a wealth of typology—should confirm that this little book is bigger than we may have thought at first glance. The genealogy discussed in the next chapter will confirm this book's significance even further.

Discussion Questions

1. Discuss the inclusio formed by Ruth 1:5 and 4:16. How has the narrative come full circle? How did the intervening events all work to bring these two verses together?

2. Whose actions are the main focus of the first part of chapter 4 (vv. 1–12)? How does this shift in focus, as well as everything we know about him, show us that Boaz is a type of Christ?

3. How does the narrator use the nearer redeemer in relation to Boaz?

4. What characteristics or circumstances of Obed make him a type of Christ, as well?

CHAPTER 7

THE GENEALOGY: JESUS AT THE CENTER OF RUTH

OPENING PRAYER: LORD JESUS CHRIST, the Word
made flesh, You revealed to Your disciples on the road
to Emmaus that all the Scriptures concern You;
open our eyes so that we may also see how all of the Law,
the Prophets, and the Writings reveal You and Your gracious
work to us; for You live and reign with the Father and
the Holy Spirit, one God, now and forever. Amen.

Introduction

THE NARRATIVE OF THE BOOK OF RUTH ends at chapter 4 verse 17. Within the world of this narrative, the narrator points us toward Yahweh's gracious work in bringing about His purposes. This rich narrative continuously demonstrates Yahweh's *chesed* and His care and concern for His people. The narrative itself also shows Jesus Christ for us through analogical prophecy and typology. The final verse of the previous section points to the truth that King David himself is a direct result of Ruth and Boaz's marriage. In the final verses, the David connection is confirmed and a connection is also made to the matriarchs and patriarchs. The genealogy helps us to move forward in time and make even more connections to the rest of Scripture.

The Genealogy in 1 Chronicles: The same genealogy also appears in a more detailed form in 1 Chronicles 2:3–15:

The sons of Judah: Er, Onan and Shelah; these three Bath-shua the
Canaanite bore to him. Now Er, Judah's firstborn, was evil in the
sight of the LORD, and He put him to death. His daughter-in-law
Tamar also bore him Perez and Zerah. Judah had five sons in all.

The sons of Perez: Hezron and Hamul. The sons of Zerah: Zimri, Ethan, Heman, Calcol, and Dara, five in all. The son of Carmi: Achan, the troubler of Israel, who broke faith in the matter of the devoted thing; and Ethan's son was Azariah.

The sons of Hezron that were born to him: Jerahmeel, Ram, and Chelubai. Ram fathered Amminadab, and Amminadab fathered Nahshon, prince of the sons of Judah. Nahshon fathered Salmon, Salmon fathered Boaz, Boaz fathered Obed, Obed fathered Jesse. Jesse fathered Eliab his firstborn, Abinadab the second, Shimea the third, Nethanel the fourth, Raddai the fifth, Ozem the sixth, David the seventh.

Verse by Verse Analysis: The Genealogy
READ CHAPTER 4:18–22

The genealogy, while brief, is rich with meaning and significance. Interestingly, it begins with Perez and not his father, Judah. This is possibly because Judah is not such an honorable link in the chain. While his is the dominant tribe and has the promise that the Messiah will come from it (see Genesis 49:10), Judah himself is conniving, adulterous, and selfish (see Genesis 38:11, 14–19, 26). Perez was the son of Tamar and Judah. As mentioned in chapter 6, Perez's birth is very interesting. He is a twin and should have been born second. However, Perez pushed his way past his brother, becoming the firstborn son and, therefore, the one with the right to the inheritance of his father. His name means "breach" because the midwife says of him, "What a breach you have made for yourself" (see Genesis 38:27–30 for the account of his birth). Perez's clan became the dominant clan in the tribe of Judah.

Perez's son, Hezron, is mentioned in a similar genealogy in Genesis 46:12. Hezron moved from Canaan to Egypt with Jacob (see Genesis 46:8, 12, 26).[53] Not much more is said of Hezron or his son, Ram. Ram's son Amminadab, however, is the father-in-law of Aaron, the first priest of Israel and the brother of Moses (see Exodus 6:23). Amminadab's son, Nahshon, is a tribe-prince of Judah during the time

---

53   See Wilch, 378.

of Moses (see Numbers 1:7; 2:3–4; and 7:12–17). Numbers 2:3–4 and 7:12–17 offer some important information about Nahshon: he was the chief of the tribes of Judah and offered the first offering in honor of the consecration of the tabernacle.

> **Numbers 2:3–4:** "Those to camp on the east side toward the sunrise shall be of the standard of the camp of Judah by their companies, the chief of the people of Judah being Nahshon the son of Amminadab, his company as listed being 74,600."

> **Numbers 7:12–17:** "He who offered his offering the first day was Nahshon the son of Amminadab, of the tribe of Judah. And his offering was one silver plate whose weight was 130 shekels, one silver basin of 70 shekels, according to the shekel of the sanctuary, both of them full of fine flour mixed with oil for a grain offering; one golden dish of 10 shekels, full of incense; one bull from the herd, one ram, one male lamb a year old, for a burnt offering; one male goat for a sin offering; and for the sacrifice of peace offerings, two oxen, five rams, five male goats, and five male lambs a year old. This was the offering of Nahshon the son of Amminadab."

According to John R. Wilch, some positions in a royal genealogy were more important than others. These are, in order of ascending importance, the fifth, seventh, and tenth positions. Nahshon is in the fifth position in this genealogy because of his importance during the time of Moses. His fame helped Judah emerge as the dominant tribe in Israel.[54] Nahshon also completes the first half of the genealogy, which covers the period from the sojourning in Egypt to the exodus. The second half covers the time of the wilderness wanderings through the monarchy.

Salmon/Salmah begins the second half of the genealogy (many biblical names have variant spellings). Matthew 1:1–6 tells us that Salmon married Rahab, the prostitute of Jericho who helped to save the Israelite spies and confessed Yahweh. Several verses in Joshua offer more information about Rahab:

---

54   Wilch, 379.

Joshua 2:8–14: "Before the men lay down, she came up to them on the roof and said to the men, 'I know that the LORD has given you the land, and that the fear of you has fallen upon us, and that all the inhabitants of the land melt away before you. For we have heard how the LORD dried up the water of the Red Sea before you when you came out of Egypt, and what you did to the two kings of the Amorites who were beyond the Jordan, to Sihon and Og, whom you devoted to destruction. And as soon as we heard it, our hearts melted, and there was no spirit left in any man because of you, for the LORD your God, He is God in the heavens above and on the earth beneath. Now then, please swear to me by the LORD that, as I have dealt kindly with you, you also will deal kindly with my father's house, and give me a sure sign that you will save alive my father and mother, my brothers and sisters, and all who belong to them, and deliver our lives from death.' And the men said to her, 'Our life for yours even to death! If you do not tell this business of ours, then when the LORD gives us the land we will deal kindly and faithfully with you.'"

Joshua 6:22–25: "But to the two men who had spied out the land, Joshua said, 'Go into the prostitute's house and bring out from there the woman and all who belong to her, as you swore to her.' So the young men who had been spies went in and brought out Rahab and her father and mother and brothers and all who belonged to her. And they brought all her relatives and put them outside the camp of Israel. And they burned the city with fire, and everything in it. Only the silver and gold, and the vessels of bronze and of iron, they put into the treasury of the house of the LORD. But Rahab the prostitute and her father's household and all who belonged to her, Joshua saved alive. And she has lived in Israel to this day, because she hid the messengers whom Joshua sent to spy out Jericho."

Like Ruth, Rahab is a foreigner who makes a bold confession of Yahweh despite the expectation that she would follow pagan gods. She and her husband are the ancestors of Boaz.[55]

Boaz is listed seventh in the genealogy. Again, this is a place of high honor; only the tenth position is more important. The events recorded in Ruth have shown Boaz to be a worthy, faithful man and an example of faithfulness to Yahweh. He is certainly an ancestor a king could be proud to have. Boaz is the biological father of Obed, although Obed was the legal heir of Mahlon and Elimelech. A child born according to Levirate marriage was an heir both of his biological father and of the man for whom he was begotten. Although Boaz and Ruth's union was not a typical Levirate marriage, Obed is considered both Elimelech's and Boaz's son. Boaz makes Obed an heir of Elimelech by proclaiming that his intention in marrying Ruth is to produce an heir to "perpetuate the name of the dead in his inheritance" (Ruth 4:5). He has to make this clear, because they are not embarking on a normal Levirate marriage: Boaz is not the brother of Elimelech or Mahlon, nor does he take Naomi, the direct person to beget an heir in Elimelech's name, as his wife, because she is too old to bear children. This more complicated scenario shows even more profoundly that Obed would have been considered the son and heir of both Elimelech and Mahlon.

Obed "fathers" Jesse (although there is probably a gap here). Jesse is mentioned both in the stories of how David came to be anointed in 1 Samuel and in some prophecies. (His name is also mentioned numerous times throughout 1 and 2 Samuel as well as the Chronicles, because David is often called "son of Jesse.") Jesse did not know or understand what his son David would become. When Samuel came to look over Jesse's sons and anoint one as king, Jesse did not call David until he was told to do so, after all of his other sons had passed before Samuel. One of the prophecies concerning the root of Jesse is in Isaiah:

---

55 Wilch has a very in-depth discussion on the chronology of this genealogy. Since it hits only the highlights, it does not list every actual person who would have been in between the more important people listed here. Salmon was probably not Boaz's father, but rather a great or great-great grandfather. The genealogy covers 850 years but lists only 10 persons. Obviously, there are some gaps here. Often in the Old Testament, an ancestor more distant than father was said to have "fathered" a grandchild, great-grandchild, or other descendant. This is still true, just not exhaustive. It was a common practice to choose the most noteworthy ancestors and condense the list. The gaps appear to be between Hezron and Ram, Salmon and Boaz, and Obed and Jesse. For a more in-depth discussion on this, see Wilch 381–2.

There shall come forth a shoot from the stump of Jesse,
    and a branch from his roots shall bear fruit.
And the Spirit of the LORD shall rest upon Him,
    the Spirit of wisdom and understanding,
    the Spirit of counsel and might,
    the Spirit of knowledge and the fear of the LORD.
And His delight shall be in the fear of the LORD.

He shall not judge by what His eyes see,
    or decide disputes by what His ears hear,
but with righteousness He shall judge the poor,
    and decide with equity for the meek of the earth;
and He shall strike the earth with the rod of His mouth,
    and with the breath of His lips He shall kill the wicked.
Righteousness shall be the belt of His waist,
    and faithfulness the belt of His loins.

The wolf shall dwell with the lamb,
    and the leopard shall lie down with the young goat,
    and the calf and the lion and the fattened calf together;
    and a little child shall lead them.
The cow and the bear shall graze;
        their young shall lie down together;
            and the lion shall eat straw like the ox.
The nursing child shall play over the hole of the cobra,
    and the weaned child shall put his hand on the adder's den.
They shall not hurt or destroy
        in all My holy mountain;
        for the earth shall be full of the knowledge of the LORD
            as the waters cover the sea.

In that day the root of Jesse, who shall stand as a signal for
the peoples—of Him shall the nations inquire, and His
resting place shall be glorious. (Isaiah 11:1–10)

This prophecy about the stump of Jesse producing a branch is clearly
a prophecy of Jesus Christ. First and foremost, though, the genealogy

as we have it in the Book of Ruth is about David, the final and tenth person mentioned in the prophecy. David occupies the prime place in this genealogy since he is the king for whom it was compiled. David was anointed by God through the prophet Samuel (who himself has a miraculous womb-opening birth) to be king over Israel. God considered David to be His son.

The genealogy includes ten names, the number of completeness. Again, this is not an exhaustive list. The genealogy highlights the most important persons leading to David and intensifies its impact for the reader. Yet, it is complete in that it traces a line from the patriarchs of Israel to David, showing both his connection to Israel's past and Yahweh's faithfulness throughout all generations.

THE GENEALOGY AS FULFILLMENT OF THE NARRATIVE

Given that the Book of Ruth is a rich and well-written narrative, the genealogy often seems out of place. But on closer examination, it fits quite well into the structure of the narrative. The Book of Ruth begins with an introduction or prologue of sorts in 1:1–5, where the narrator offers us the background to the story he is about to tell. He relates the near extinction of Elimelech's family. All that is left is Naomi— just one person, and a woman! Surely Elimelech's family will disappear from the earth. In those first five verses, we have an account of three rather faithless men, who chose to at least temporarily cash in Yahweh's gift and travel among pagans to live and work. While the conclusion in 4:1–17 brings this full circle by relating how faithful Boaz and faithful Ruth conceive a son, Obed, in Elimelech's name, the genealogy takes this one step further. By giving a bigger picture of the family tree in which Obed, Boaz, and Ruth fit, the narrator offers a fitting epilogue to balance the prologue of the first five verses of the book. This epilogue takes us both backward and forward in time. Elimelech's family will not die out; in fact it will flourish! A king will come forth from it! And it is through Boaz's ancestry that the connection is made with the patriarchs, as well. This connection has previously been stressed in the Book of Ruth through prayers, blessings, and similar events and through circumstances in the narrative that correlate with those of the patriarchs and matriarchs (for instance, the betrothal type-scene). By moving backward to the patriarchs and forward to King David, the narrator shows how the Book of Ruth fits into the overall arc of Israel's history. It is through the strange individual events of the lives of Ruth, Naomi, and Boaz that Yahweh continues to act on His promise of a Seed, a promise made to the patriarchs and matriarchs and reiterated to Judah for the benefit of all Israelites. The genealogy helps the hearer to understand the full significance of the book and why it is important that it be heard again and again. It is sort of like a movie camera pulling out from a close-up to show the bigger picture. The Book of Ruth is not just about Ruth: it is about all Israelites, all believers, all members of God's chosen people. And it is about Yahweh working to fulfill His promises.

THE GENEALOGY AS FULFILLMENT OF THE PRAYERS OF THE BOOK OF RUTH

The genealogy also underscores the fact that all of the prayers or blessings in the Book of Ruth are fulfilled by the end of the book. This is important because Yahweh is less obviously involved in Ruth than in Old Testament narratives like Genesis or Exodus. The narrator purposely shows that the prayers and blessings are answered to make the point that it is Yahweh, whether or not we see Him explicitly at work, who both inspires the prayers and blessings and fulfills them. Here are some of the specific prayers or blessings in Ruth that are partially fulfilled in the genealogy (more are fulfilled in the narrative proper, but we will look here at those most closely connected with the genealogy).

"THE LORD REPAY YOU . . . "

In Ruth 2:12, Boaz asks a blessing on Ruth: "The LORD repay you for what you have done, and a full reward be given you by the LORD, the God of Israel, under whose wings you have come to take refuge!" This verse is fulfilled in chapter 4 when Ruth becomes a wife and conceives a child. She has truly been repaid for her kindnesses to her mother-in-law, and she has been given a "full reward" through the gift of a child and a place in the lineage of a king.

"Blessed be the man . . ."

Again, this brief prayer from Naomi upon finding out what Boaz did for Ruth (2:19) is fulfilled in part through the genealogy. Boaz is blessed by Yahweh as a father, and as a member of the lineage of King David and beyond.

"May the Lord make the woman . . . like Rachel and Leah."

In Ruth 4:11–12, in response to Boaz's sacrifice and work on Ruth and Naomi's behalf, the people of Bethlehem pronounce a blessing upon Boaz and Ruth: "We are witnesses. May the Lord make the woman, who is coming into your house, like Rachel and Leah, who together built up the house of Israel. May you act worthily in Ephrathah and be renowned in Bethlehem, and may your house be like the house of Perez, whom Tamar bore to Judah, because of the offspring that the Lord will give you by this young woman." This particular blessing has several aspects and several fulfillments. First, the desire for Ruth to be like Rachel and Leah and to have offspring is fulfilled in the birth of Obed. In this way, Ruth builds up the house of both Boaz and Elimelech, since the child is heir of both men. The genealogy takes this a step further: Ruth is connected to the matriarchs through Perez (whose very name is mentioned in this blessing!). Obed, identified as Boaz's son and not Elimelech's for the purposes of the genealogy, is connected to the tribe of Judah, the dominant tribe in all of Israel. Boaz's further offspring through Ruth are also emphasized by the genealogy. Not only did Boaz father Obed as a fulfillment of this blessing, but his lineage reaches to King David, so his offspring continues to be important, integral to Israel's life, and impressive. Additionally, the wish that Boaz's name be renowned in Bethlehem is fulfilled by the people's speaking this blessing and by his son Obed's communal naming. The genealogy confirms his renown by including him among those specially selected to show David's lineage and by his seventh position in the genealogy, second only to David. In this way the genealogy confirms Boaz's renown beyond just Bethlehem and Ephrathah.

"Blessed be the Lord . . .

and may his [Obed's] name be renowned in Israel!"

The women pronounce a final blessing on Naomi in Ruth 4:14–15. They pray: "Blessed be the Lord, who has not left you this day without a redeemer, and may his name be renowned in Israel! He shall be to you a restorer of life and a nourisher of your old age, for your daughter-in-law who loves you, who is more to you than seven sons, has given birth to him." This blessing is fulfilled, first, in the communal naming of Obed. The fact that he is named by the entire community makes his name already renowned or famous. Naomi is nourished and restored when he is laid in her lap. The genealogy confirms the renown of Obed's name by including him in the ancestry of David. As an ancestor of David, Obed's name will be renowned throughout all time and in all of Israel.

THE GENEALOGY AS FULFILLMENT
OF THE PURPOSE OF THE BOOK

If we think back to the first chapter of this book and our discussion of the purposes of the Book of Ruth, the genealogy makes a lot of sense. One of the purposes of Ruth was to legitimate David's rule and some of the practices of his kingship (such as the admission of foreigners to the assembly of God's people). Remember, David was nowhere near a direct heir to the kingship. In the eyes of some, Saul's sons were the proper holders of the rule of Israel and Judah by virtue of the fact that they were Saul's sons; in other words, by virtue of their genealogy. The need to legitimate David over Saul's sons is demonstrated by the attempted coup in 2 Samuel 2 (just one instance of the ongoing fight between the house of Saul and the house of David; see also 2 Samuel 3). For a time, Ish-bosheth, a son of Saul, rules over part of the Divided Kingdom (Israel) while David rules over the other (Judah). This is because Abner, the commander of Saul's army, makes Ish-bosheth king over Israel. He does this of his own volition and not out of the will of God. Israel follows Ish-bosheth for two years (2 Samuel 2:8–11). This begins to disintegrate when the armies of David and Abner fight at Gibeon (2 Samuel 2:12–32) and then David defeats them. So it is clear from this story that many in Israel believed the rule belonged not to David, but to a direct heir of Saul. Yet God chose David—a shepherd boy and the youngest of the eight sons of Jesse—and not a son of King Saul. For some, David's worthiness for and right to the throne needed to be qualified in human terms, even though God Himself had chosen him. Therefore, David needs a genealogy worthy of a king. The genealogy, then, affirms one of the main purposes of telling Ruth, Naomi, and Boaz's story in the first place. Given that David has such honorable ancestors, he is worthy of the kingship.

As the genealogy caps the narrative, the history of David's ancestors Ruth and Boaz lends weight both to his worthiness to be king and to the worthiness of some foreigners to be a part of Israel. Ruth's clear worthiness, her confession of Yahweh as Lord, and her acceptance by the people of Bethlehem demonstrate a precedent for foreigners to be accepted into the assembly of Israel, even those whose people, like Ruth's, were specifically forbidden to enter into the Lord's sanctuary until the tenth generation (see Deuteronomy 23:3). The genealogy, then, defends David's kingship and further shows the impact of this short story in the history of Israel. This is how Yahweh works: He not only serves, protects, and saves individuals like Naomi and Ruth, He also serves, protects, and saves all people. These two activities are combined in the Book of Ruth. By saving this family, Yahweh saves the nation of Israel by bringing forth King David from their offspring. Yet, there is more to the genealogy than David.

THE GENEALOGY IN THE NEW TESTAMENT

Now that we have seen the significance of the genealogy in Ruth and its connection to other parts of the Old Testament, we can consider its impact for the New Testament and its further use. This genealogy is quoted nearly word for word in the Gospel of Matthew:

> The book of the genealogy of Jesus Christ, the son of David, the son of Abraham.
>
> Abraham was the father of Isaac, and Isaac the father of Jacob, and Jacob the father of Judah and his brothers, and Judah the father of Perez and Zerah by Tamar, and Perez the father of Hezron, and

Hezron the father of Ram, and Ram the father of Amminadab, and Amminadab the father of Nahshon, and Nahshon the father of Salmon, and Salmon the father of Boaz by Rahab, and Boaz the father of Obed by Ruth, and Obed the father of Jesse, and Jesse the father of David the king. (Matthew 1:1–6a)

Notice that Matthew begins with Abraham, the one who was promised that the Messiah would come from his family and that his descendants would be as numerous as the stars (Genesis 15). Matthew also includes two women specifically in this part of his genealogy: Rahab and Ruth. Both were, of course, believing foreign women. Here, their inclusion foreshadows the fact that Jesus has come not just for the Israelites, but for all people, including the Gentiles.

Matthew's genealogy continues:

And David was the father of Solomon by the wife of Uriah, and Solomon the father of Rehoboam, and Rehoboam the father of Abijah, and Abijah the father of Asaph, and Asaph the father of Jehoshaphat, and Jehoshaphat the father of Joram, and Joram the father of Uzziah, and Uzziah the father of Jotham, and Jotham the father of Ahaz, and Ahaz the father of Hezekiah, and Hezekiah the father of Manasseh, and Manasseh the father of Amos, and Amos the father of Josiah, and Josiah the father of Jechoniah and his brothers, at the time of the deportation to Babylon.

And after the deportation to Babylon: Jechoniah was the father of Shealtiel, and Shealtiel the father of Zerubbabel, and Zerubbabel the father of Abiud, and Abiud the father of Eliakim, and Eliakim the father of Azor, and Azor the father of Zadok, and Zadok the father of Achim, and Achim the father of Eliud, and Eliud the father of Eleazar, and Eleazar the father of Matthan, and Matthan the father of Jacob, and Jacob the father of Joseph the husband of Mary, of whom Jesus was born, who is called Christ.

So all the generations from Abraham to David were fourteen generations, and from David to the deportation to Babylon fourteen generations, and from the deportation to Babylon to the Christ fourteen generations. (Matthew 1:6–17)

According to Matthew's genealogy, then, the ultimate Seed of Abraham is Jesus Christ. Paul also confesses this in Galatians 3:16, 19, and 29:

Now the promises were made to Abraham and to his offspring. It does not say, "And to offsprings," referring to many, but referring to one, "And to your offspring," who is Christ. . . . Why then the law? It was added because of transgressions, until the offspring should come to whom the promise had been made, and it was put in place through angels by an intermediary. . . . And if you are Christ's, then you are Abraham's offspring, heirs according to promise.

In connection with Matthew's extension of it, the genealogy of the Book of Ruth points us forward to Jesus Christ, the one even greater than David, who was to come to fulfill the promise given by Yahweh to Eve, Abraham, Isaac, and Jacob. The events and people of Ruth who point us forward to Jesus through analogical prophecy and typology are supported by this genealogy and its connection to the New Testament genealogy in Matthew. Yahweh worked through Ruth, Boaz, and Naomi—through famine and feast, through laws concerning kinsman-redeemers and Levirate marriage, through conception and birth, and through journeys and homecomings—to bring about His purposes for Ruth and Naomi, for King David, and finally for King Jesus and us.

INTERPRETATION: JESUS AT THE CENTER OF THE BOOK OF RUTH

We have arrived at Jesus in the Book of Ruth through analogical prophecy and typology and through genealogy. The Book of Ruth is really about Jesus. It is not first and foremost about us (although, since we are in Christ, it *becomes* about us in a unique way). It is not primarily about what Ruth as a person might teach us. It is not even primarily about Ruth.

The Book of Ruth is primarily about Jesus. He is at once its subject, its object, and its fulfillment.

Indeed, Jesus is the subject, object, and fulfillment of all of the Scriptures. He points this out Himself when He appears to His disciples in His resurrected form on the road to Emmaus (Luke 24:13–35). All of the Scriptures (here Jesus is referring to the Law, the Prophets, and the Writings of the Old Testament, since those were the only Scriptures in existence at that point) are ultimately about Jesus. As He opens their eyes, the disciples are amazed at the revelation He has given them. Therefore, we have it on the authority of Jesus' own words that all of the Scriptures are about Him. The Book of Ruth connects to Jesus through prophecy, typology, genealogy, prayers, and more.

Jesus and the Theme of Emptiness and Fulfillment

Jesus is the fulfillment of even the themes and motifs in the Book of Ruth. One of the first themes that comes to the fore in the narrative is that of emptiness and fullness. The prologue begins by leaving Naomi empty. She herself, later in the narrative, laments that she "went away full," but has returned "empty" (Ruth 1:21). All of this was brought about by God's hand. Over the course of the narrative, He works in stages to bring fullness to Naomi: He provides Ruth, He brings them back home at harvest time so they have sustenance, He makes sure Ruth meets Boaz, He makes circumstances favorable for Boaz and Ruth to marry, and finally He opens Ruth's womb and provides a child as a provider for her future. By chapter 4, Naomi has come full circle from being empty of all things—children, house, land, husband, food—to being full, with a place in Boaz and Ruth's home, the return of her husband's land, and a child in her old age.

God doesn't stop there. Through the child He has placed on Naomi's lap, Yahweh provides not just this nearer redeemer, but also the ultimate Redeemer, His very own Son. Through the promise and the coming of the Promised One, God provides Naomi with forgiveness, life, hope, joy, peace, and rest. He does this for us too! Naomi's fullness is our fullness. Like Naomi, we are empty when we come into the "House of Bread," God's Church on earth. We come as sinners drowned in the depth of death, sin, the world, our flesh, and the devil. We come with nothing to offer. Yet Yahweh draws us in and fills us with forgiveness, life, and salvation. He fills us in our Baptism with His own name and His forgiveness and promises. He fills us in the Lord's Supper with bread and wine, Christ's own body and blood. Indeed, even when we are bereft of job, house, family, children, health, wealth, or even hope, our Lord God continues to work to fill us. In Christ we are already full, although that fullness may not be realized until He comes again.

Jesus and the *Chesed* of Yahweh

A major focus in the narrative of Ruth is Yahweh's *chesed*, or loving-kindness and faithfulness. This is seen both in confessions made concerning Yahweh's characteristic of *chesed* and in the actions of Ruth and Boaz, who live out Yahweh's *chesed* in their service to others and their faithfulness to God. Jesus is the subject (in other words, the doer of the verb) with regard to *chesed*, because He is the one who perfectly lives it out. Jesus is perfectly faithful to Yahweh; therefore He shows the *chesed* of Yahweh. His faithfulness extends to Him showing *chesed* to the whole world. Like Ruth and Boaz, who foreshadow Him, Jesus goes above and beyond the Law to serve His neighbors—all people through all time. Jesus loves us with *chesed*. He shows loving-kindness and faithfulness to us even in the midst of our hard-heartedness and unfaithfulness. Ultimately, He demonstrates His *chesed* by dying on the cross for our sins so that we may become the beloved children of God, objects of His eternal *chesed*.

Jesus is also the object of God the Father's *chesed*. At His Baptism and during the transfiguration, God declares Jesus to be His beloved Son. Even when Jesus' body lies in the grave, broken and killed because of the sins of the whole world, even after abandoning Him to hell, God remains faithful to Jesus and raises Him from the dead. He exalts Jesus to the heavenly places as Lord of all.

Finally, Jesus is the fulfillment of Yahweh's *chesed* and of the typological *chesed* shown by Ruth and Boaz. Ruth and Boaz show Yahweh's *chesed* by going above and beyond the Law for the sake of their neighbor (for Ruth this is Naomi; for Boaz this is Ruth and Naomi). Jesus is the fulfillment of Ruth and Boaz's types. As types, their lives prophesy about Jesus, and Jesus fulfills those prophecies. He is the one who loves perfectly both God and neighbor. Jesus is the fulfillment of Yahweh's *chesed*, because He is the one through whom Yahweh ultimately shows His loving-kindness and faithfulness to the world. The *chesed* Yahweh has shown to His chosen people throughout the Old Testament culminates in Jesus.

JESUS AND THE THEME OF THE REMNANT

In Ruth, Naomi is left as the faithful remnant of her family (her faithfulness is shown by her prayers for her daughters-in-law). Her state as one who is left is a part of the overall theme of the remnant throughout the Old Testament. In the Book of Ruth, Naomi is left, and then Ruth joins her as the remnant of the faithful from Elimelech's family. Throughout the narrative, Yahweh works to increase the remnant. The birth of Obed—whose name means "servant" or "worshiper"—points to further faithful members of Ruth and Naomi's family growing this remnant. In Isaiah and the prophets, the idea of God leaving just a remnant from which His promised Seed will come is explored over and over again as He deals with the rebellion and unbelief of the majority of the Israelites. In each grouping, He preserves a remnant from which He will draw His faithful people and, in His time, the Messiah. When we come to the New Testament, Jesus is Israel reduced to one. He is the faithful remnant in all of God's house. He alone is completely faithful to Yahweh. Through Jesus, all those baptized into His death and resurrection become the faithful remnant with Him and are gathered to God the Father as His people.

JESUS AS THE FULFILLMENT OF THE DAVID PURPOSE

While the human writer of Ruth had in mind human purposes for defending David and showing his lineage, Yahweh's divine purposes are revealed through the writer's purposes. They do so first of all because David was Yahweh's chosen and anointed king of Israel. However, in a very real way, Jesus is the fulfillment of the purpose of Ruth with regard to defending David as king. While David was the earthly king and anointed one of God, Jesus is the King of heaven and earth, anointed by God the Father. Like David, Jesus invites foreigners into the assembly of God. All believers in Christ are a part of the congregation of God. Matthew makes this point very clearly when he includes Rahab and Ruth in the genealogy of Jesus. (Not even the narrator of Ruth is bold enough to include the women's names in the genealogy.) Matthew foreshadows some of what his Gospel will show about Jesus: He came for all of the lost, not just the lost sheep of Israel. The inclusion of foreigners begins with the wise men from distant lands who come to worship the infant Jesus (Matthew 2:1ff). It is buoyed by the story of the Roman centurion's faith (Matthew 8), the Canaanite woman who asks for healing for her demon-oppressed daughter (Matthew 15:21–28), and the centurion (and others with him) at the foot of the cross who confesses that Jesus was surely "the Son of God" (Matthew 27:54). While David is notable in the Old Testament for including believing foreigners, it is through Jesus' life, death, and resurrection that people of all ethnicities become children of God. He calls all nations into His genealogy to partake of His inheritance and kingdom, by Baptism and Word.

Finally, like David, Jesus is the beloved Son of God (but Jesus is all of these things and does all of these things in a more perfect and complete way than David). David's genealogy is Jesus' genealogy. David's worthy ancestors are Jesus' worthy ancestors. In the end, Jesus is the King for whom the patriarchs and matriarchs waited and whose second coming the world now awaits. He is the true fulfillment of the genealogy of Ruth.

JESUS AS THE FULFILLMENT OF THE PRAYERS OF RUTH

Truly, Jesus fulfills all the prayers in that it is through Him and His intercession that all prayers are brought to God the Father. However, some prayers in the Book of Ruth are very clearly and specifically fulfilled by Jesus.

"REST IN THE HOUSE OF YOUR HUSBAND"

The first prayer in the Book of Ruth is spoken by Naomi for her two daughters-in-law at the beginning of the narrative as she makes her way home from Moab. She tells Orpah and Ruth to return to their parents and asks that Yahweh "deal kindly with you, as you have dealt with the dead and with me. The LORD grant that you may find rest, each of you in the house of her husband!" (1:8–9). Orpah goes home, and Ruth, as we know, stays with Naomi. Naomi's prayer is fulfilled for Ruth throughout the narrative as Yahweh, through the barley harvest and through Boaz, "deals kindly" with her. Indeed, Ruth finds rest in the house of her husband as a wife and mother, and she partakes in the rest given to God's covenant people.

Ultimately, the fulfillment of the promised rest, the Sabbath rest, is Jesus Christ. Jesus is the Lord of the Sabbath and, therefore, is the Lord of rest. He brings God's promised Sabbath rest to us. The commandment tells us to keep the Sabbath holy because it is a day of rest that our Creator has set aside for us. Since we cannot keep the Law perfectly, our Sabbaths often are not restful or holy. It is Jesus who fulfills this Law for us, keeps the Sabbath holy, and promises Sabbath rest.

Over and over again in the Gospels, Jesus shows that He is the Lord of the Sabbath by defying the extra laws the Pharisees had devised about the day. To be absolutely sure they did not break God's commandment, the Jewish leaders had invented numerous laws to try to build a hedge around the commandments. These man-made laws obscured the purpose of God's commandment in the first place: that His people might find rest in Him and His service to them on the Sabbath day. Instead, they made the Sabbath another kind of work such that it became an anxiety-ridden burden rather than a joyful, peaceful rest. Several times in the Gospels, the Pharisees and Sadducees confront Jesus about what they consider a sin against the commandment (every time Jesus heals someone on the Sabbath, this is a problem for them):

> One Sabbath He was going through the grainfields, and as they made their way, His disciples began to pluck heads of grain. And the Pharisees were saying to Him, "Look, why are they doing what is not lawful on the Sabbath?" And He said to them, "Have you never read what David did, when he was in need and was hungry, he and those who were with him: how he entered the house of God, in the time of Abiathar the high priest, and ate the bread of the Presence, which it is not lawful for any but the priests to eat, and also gave it to those who were with him?" And He said to them, "The Sabbath was made for man, not man for the Sabbath. So the Son of Man is lord even of the Sabbath." (Mark 2:23–28)

Here, Jesus' disciples pluck grain to eat as they journey. To the Pharisees, this was work and a violation of the Sabbath. But Jesus' point is that the disciples are hungry and must eat. The point of the Sabbath command to rest from our labors is not to terrify or to leave people to starve if they have no food prepared. He shows them the truth that the Sabbath is made for us and is a gift from God to us to restore us and give us time to rest from our labors.

Notice the interesting parallel Jesus makes here between the disciples eating the heads of grain and David eating the bread of the Presence. The bread of the Presence was an Old Testament precursor to the New Testament gift of Jesus' body in the Lord's Supper. Truly the bread of the Lord's Supper is the real bread of the Presence. In comparing the disciples' actions to David's, Jesus makes two points: the bread of the Presence is for everyone, not just the priests, and our daily bread of grain, meat, and fruits and vegetables is linked to our other daily bread, Christ's presence for us in the Lord's Supper.

Jesus shows us that the Sabbath rest is made for us, not as a burden to be kept, but as a gift to be enjoyed, wherein we can revel in God's presence and service to us through Word and Sacrament. Because the Sabbath is a gift from Him, we ought to keep it, to be in the Word, and to reflect it in what we say and do. In fact, Jesus also shows that *He* is our Sabbath rest. He is the one who gives us our rest:

> All things have been handed over to Me by My Father, and no
> one knows the Son except the Father, and no one knows the Father
> except the Son and anyone to whom the Son chooses to reveal
> Him. Come to Me, all who labor and are heavy laden, and I will give
> you rest. Take My yoke upon you, and learn from Me, for I am gentle and lowly in heart, and you will find rest for your souls. For My
> yoke is easy, and My burden is light. (Matthew 11:27–30)

Jesus gives us our Sabbath rest. In Him all people find their rest, which means that Jesus is the ultimate fulfillment of Naomi's prayer that Ruth find rest. As a believer and confessor of Yahweh, Ruth receives from Jesus all His gifts, including the gift of resting in Him for all eternity.

"THE LORD REPAY YOU . . . " (2:12)

Boaz asks this blessing over Ruth when he meets her in the fields. He asks that the Lord repay her for her kindness to Naomi and give her a reward. This is an interesting choice of words. Abraham was promised a reward from God: "After these things the word of the LORD came to Abram in a vision: 'Fear not, Abram, I am your shield; your reward shall be very great'" (Genesis 15:1). Yahweh then reiterates His promise to Abraham that his own son will be his heir, and that his family will be too numerous to count. The hearers of the Book of Ruth probably would have made a connection between a "reward" and an "heir" because of Genesis 15. Of course, the heir of Abraham, Isaac, was a gift given by God not just for Abraham but also for the whole world. As Wilch points out, the reward of the heir is not for Abraham's sake or for Ruth's sake, but for the sake of Jesus. Ruth, too, will have an heir as her reward, and that heir is of course a precursor to the ultimate heir: Jesus Christ, who comes to save all people from their sins.[56] So while Boaz's prayer for a reward is immediately fulfilled by an heir, Obed, given to Ruth by Yahweh, it is also about the heir, Jesus Christ, who is Ruth's very great reward, and indeed, our very great reward as well.

"MAY THE LORD MAKE THE WOMAN . . . LIKE RACHEL AND LEAH" (4:11–12)

As discussed above, this prayer is first fulfilled in the Book of Ruth when Ruth helps to build up Boaz's house by giving birth to Obed, who would be an ancestor of King David. Surely to bear a king is the fulfillment of this prayer that Ruth be like Rachel and Leah in building up the house of Israel and that Boaz's family become as important as Perez's. Yet there is a further fulfillment of this prayer in Christ Jesus. It is through Him that God ultimately builds up the house of Israel; that is, it is through Him that God calls, enlightens, saves, and sanctifies His chosen people. The Church is the new Israel, which is built up by Jesus' death and resurrection, through His Word and Sacraments. Baptism makes disciples by gifting God's children with faith and bringing them into the family of God, thereby building up God's house. The Lord's Supper is the family meal where the family body is strengthened in faith toward God and in love and service toward one another. The preached Word continuously kills and makes alive through Law and Gospel in order to make God's family one of repentance, forgiveness, and love.

Additionally, Jesus is the fulfillment and ultimate expression of

---

56   See Wilch, 224.

Boaz's renown, because his name will be known throughout all time as an ancestor of Jesus, the Messiah. Jesus' name is honored above all other names, thereby fulfilling the women's prayer that Boaz be renowned. Furthermore, Jesus is *the* offspring ultimately brought about through Ruth as one in the lineage of Christ. Truly, Jesus fulfills every aspect of this blessing.

"BLESSED BE THE LORD . . . AND MAY HIS [OBED'S] NAME BE RENOWNED IN ISRAEL!" (4:14–15)

In this final prayer, the women ask that Obed's name be renowned in Israel, and they bless Naomi by saying that Obed will be a nourisher of her old age and a restorer of life. In his role as the now nearest kinsman-redeemer, Obed is all of these things. Jesus is even more completely all of these things. Jesus' renown fulfills the renown of Obed's name. Jesus is the complete nourisher of Naomi, and He is the one who will ultimately restore her life. Since Jesus is "the resurrection and the life" (see John 11), Jesus is the one who finally fulfills the blessing that the women pronounce on Naomi. Jesus is our refresher and our life-giver as well. He provides us with all we need for body and soul (see Luther's explanation of the Lord's Prayer in the Small Catechism). He raises us up from death on the Last Day, thereby restoring our lives along with Naomi's.

IT IS ABOUT YOU, AFTER ALL

In the introduction, I said this book wasn't about you. And it still isn't, at least not in a popular "life application," "principles of living" kind of way. Likewise, the Book of Ruth still is not about how to be a better woman. It still isn't about how to strive to be like Ruth, about how to take situations from Ruth's life and apply them to our own. For instance, Elimelech, Mahlon, and Chilion's apparent punishment for leaving home is not a lesson to all people about not moving to a foreign country or even just another town or state because we are not bound to the land as Old Testament believers were. It isn't an excuse to say, "Oh, I'm being punished just like they were." Why? Because Ruth isn't about how our lives compare to those of Ruth, Naomi, Boaz, Mahlon, or Chilion. Ruth isn't about our strivings. It isn't a hotbed of principles for living.

Ruth is about Jesus.

Therefore, Ruth is about us.

It is about Jesus for us. It is about Yahweh working tirelessly throughout all generations to deliver Jesus to us. The Book of Ruth is a wonderful picture of how God watches carefully over every little detail so His grace may come to fruition and fully abound. And this history is just one link in a long chain of carefully orchestrated individual lives brought together for Yahweh to carry out His gracious plan for the redemption of the earth and all mankind: Jesus Christ and Him crucified. Ruth is about the culmination of this ever-faithful loving-kindness of Yahweh (His *chesed*) in Jesus Christ, the ultimate expression of that *chesed*.

A Few Other "Image of God" Verses:

In the beginning, Adam and Eve were made in the image of God. Part of the image of God is holiness, blessedness, and righteousness. And in the fall, this was lost to us. However, in Christ, the image of God is restored, and we are again made in His image.

Genesis 1:26–27: "Then God said, 'Let Us make man in Our image, after Our likeness. And let them have dominion over the fish of the sea and over the birds of the heavens and over the livestock and over all the earth and over every creeping thing that creeps on the earth.' So God created man in His own image, in the image of God He created him; male and female He created them."

Interestingly, Genesis makes a point of saying that Adam's children are begotten in *his* image, implying that they now inherit something from him rather than from God.

Genesis 5:3: "When Adam had lived 130 years, he fathered a son in his own likeness, after his image, and named him Seth."

1 Corinthians 15:49: "Just as we have borne the image of the man of dust, we shall also bear the image of the man of heaven."

2 Corinthians 3:12–18: "Since we have such a hope, we are very bold, not like Moses, who would put a veil over his face so that the Israelites might not gaze at the outcome of what was being brought to an end. But their minds were hardened. For to this day, when they read the old covenant, that same veil remains unlifted, because only through Christ is it taken away. Yes, to this day whenever Moses is read a veil lies over their hearts. But when one turns to the Lord, the veil is removed. Now the Lord is the Spirit, and where the Spirit of the Lord is, there is freedom. And we all, with unveiled face, beholding the glory of the Lord, are being transformed into the same image from one degree of glory to another. For this comes from the Lord who is the Spirit."

There are more examples of verses concerning the image of God and who has it (first Jesus, then us!). These verses offer an overview that moves from having the image, to losing it, to its restoration. As those who are being made into Christ's image, we already are blessed, righteous, and holy.

In addition, the Book of Ruth is about us because it is about Jesus for us in our strivings. Rather than *strive* to be like Ruth, we know that God is already *molding* us to be like Ruth. How? God calls, enlightens, and sanctifies us by His Holy Spirit through His Word of Law and Gospel. This word and activity of the Holy Spirit is constantly remaking us, even killing us so that we die to self and then raising us to live to God over and over and over again. We are constantly being made into Christ's image: "For those whom He foreknew He also predestined to be conformed to the image of His Son, in order that He might be the firstborn among many brothers" (Romans 8:29). Therefore, since Ruth is a type of Christ, we are in a sense also Ruths in that we are being made into the image of Christ through the cruciform life. We may not see it, we may not notice the progress, it may even seem to us that we've taken two steps forward and one step back, but the Holy Spirit at work in us does not measure things by appearances, but by declarations. God has declared us to be His beloved children, therefore, we are already just like *the* beloved Child of God: His only Son, Jesus Christ. When we stand in our Baptisms, that is to say, when Jesus stands in for us by virtue of the fact that we are baptized into His name, there is no backward or forward in God's eyes, no more or less holy, no progress or regress. There are only truths and promises and declarations and holiness and righteousness and blessedness and wholeness. There is only Jesus. And Jesus places His wings over you, and He covers you with His identity—that of beloved Child of God. He is your Levir and your kinsman-redeemer, your rest and your daily bread. You are His image and workmanship, already perfect and complete in God's eyes through His Son. And that is what Ruth is all about.

Discussion Questions

1. Here is a chart showing all of the blessings in the Book of Ruth. Find each blessing and then complete the chart by briefly showing how it is fulfilled either within the Book of Ruth, beyond the Book of Ruth, and/or in Jesus.

Blessing	Fulfillment in Ruth	Fulfillment beyond Ruth	Fulfillment in Jesus
Ruth 1:8–9			
Ruth 2:4			
Ruth 2:12			
Ruth 2:19			
Ruth 3:10			
Ruth 4:11–12			
Ruth 4:14–15			

2. How is the genealogy a fitting capstone for the Book of Ruth?

3. How does the genealogy point us forward to David and then to Christ?

4. What are the different ways in which the Book of Ruth has shown us Jesus in some way?

APPENDIX A

Answer Guides for Discussion Questions

CHAPTER 1:

1. Given the discussion of prophesy by way of typology or analogy, what are some other Old Testament scriptural events or persons that point forward to Christ and His gifts?

   Typology is an especially rich and often well-covered category of how the Old Testament prophesies Christ through persons who are like Him in personality and situation. Some types of Christ include:

   Moses: *Moses speaks with God "mouth to mouth" (Numbers 3:7–8). The only person with more access to God than Moses had is Christ, who sees the Father face-to-face. Moses is God's prophet, probably the greatest prophet of the Old Testament. Jesus is the Prophet of God, even greater than Moses. Moses is also called the most humble or meek man (Numbers 12:7–8). Jesus, the God-man who does not make use of His divine power when upon the cross but empties Himself to become obedient to death (Philippians 2:1–11), is ultimately the most humble and meek man. Moses intercedes for the Israelites; Jesus is our intercessor. (See the Book of Hebrews for several different references to how Moses was a type of Christ that Christ Himself has fulfilled and outdone, for example, Hebrews 3 and 8.)*

   David: *David was the King of Israel and God's chosen anointed. God often refers to him as His son and as someone after God's own heart. David sang psalms to the Lord, obeyed and trusted in Him, and was anointed by the Lord through the prophet Samuel (see 1 Samuel 16, esp. vv.11–13). However, David made major mistakes and had many issues as a king and as a person. Jesus is our King, and He is the Son of David, but He fulfills and goes beyond David's life as a King, and He is a better King than David.*

Jesus rules perfectly, lived a perfect life, truly is God's Son, is THE Anointed One (that is what the title "Christ" means), and is not just David's son, but also David's Lord (Matthew 22:41–46). Additionally, Jesus often prayed the psalms of David and fulfilled all of the prophecies about Him contained in David's psalms (as well as other psalms).

The Bible also often prophesies of Christ analogically, or by analogy. It does this through events in the history of Israel or specific events in the lives of Old Testament persons that point forward to specific events or actions that will occur in Jesus' lifetime or as a result of His death and resurrection.

The sacrifice of Isaac (Genesis 22): Isaac is a type of Christ when he is being taken to Mount Moriah to be sacrificed by Abraham. The event of the sacrifice of Isaac is an event that analogically prophesies God's sacrifice of His Son, Jesus, and Jesus' willingness to go to the cross. Jesus is the Lamb of God provided by Yahweh Himself for the salvation of His people. Like Isaac, Jesus trusts His Father's will and obeys silently (see John's account of the crucifixion, especially John 19:9 and Isaiah 53:7). There is no struggle from Isaac when Abraham lays Isaac upon the altar to sacrifice him. In the same way, Jesus goes forward willingly to the cross and lays down His life upon that altar, becoming the ultimate sacrifice for the sins of the whole world. Yahweh provides Jesus, the Lamb of God, as the final sacrifice, so that "at the right time, Christ died for the ungodly" (Romans 5:6).

The exodus: The exodus is another example of an event that prophesies analogically about Christ's life or work. Yahweh leads His chosen people to freedom and safety from Egyptian slavery. Similarly, Christ Himself leads us out of the slavery of sin, death, and the devil, and into the freedom of being His children.

The people of Israel and the wilderness: Jesus is also Israel reduced to one person. God has made Jesus the chosen Son, and in Him the rest of God's people are finally chosen. Like He led the Israelites into and then out of the wilderness during the exo-

dus wanderings, He also led Jesus into the wilderness to face the temptation of the devil (which Jesus faced perfectly, unlike the Israelites, who grumbled, complained, and sinned against God during the wilderness wanderings) and then called Him back out of the wilderness.

These are just a few examples of both typology and analogical prophecy in the Old Testament. See Luke 9 for an example from the New Testament.

2. Recall the discussion about Elimelech and his relationship to the patriarchs. How was Elimelech's situation different than that of the patriarchs? How did Elimelech's actions demonstrate a lack of faith? What are some situations or life experiences that might present us with the same dilemma as Elimelech in prompting a lack of trust in God our Father?

Elimelech was not given a command from God to sojourn in a distant land as were the patriarchs discussed in this chapter (e.g., Abraham, Isaac). Although the patriarchs did sojourn during famines, they were often commanded to do so by God. Additionally, at the time of the patriarchs' sojourns, Yahweh had not yet given them the Promised Land as He had by the time Elimelech left for Moab. Elimelech gave up God's gift of the land, a gift that was understood as a foretaste and precursor of the gift of eternal life and salvation as one of God's chosen people, and left it behind. In other words, he showed a certain amount of disdain for God's gift and a definite mistrust in both Yahweh's ability to provide and His gracious will to do so.

Some times when we might be tempted to leave behind or disregard Yahweh's gifts to us might be when doubts plague us, our faith weakens, and we are tempted to walk away from our faith, essentially saying to God, "Here is the gift of life, faith, and salvation that you gave me in my Baptism so graciously. I reject it. I no longer want it. Thanks, but no thanks." Another time this might happen is when we are tempted to stay away from the Lord's house when there are opportunities for regular worship.

Here again, we are saying to God, "Your gifts of Christ's body and blood, of forgiveness, life, and salvation, are not as important to me as sleeping in, sports, or work." When we act this way, we often do not trust in God's gifts to help us in our lives as much as we trust in work, sleeping, or some other pursuit or mindset. (Certain professions and jobs may offer no choice but to work on Sunday. In these cases, try to find a Saturday service or schedule a time to meet with your pastor about private Confession and Absolution and a Communion visit for those weeks when you are unable to attend).

Finally, a situation similar to Elimelech's that may cause us doubt or mistrust might be the death of a loved one or the loss of a job, income, or house. These things can be very much like our own personal famines. We may be tempted to pursue other avenues of support or help that are not God-pleasing or just forget that God is waiting to provide, though it may not be obvious how and it may not happen as quickly as we wish. The fact that a loved one has died or that a job comes to an end does not mean that we are being punished in some specific way. It only means that we live in a fallen world. The situations do present us with challenges wherein we might make choices like Elimelech's, but God is always with us in these times and is ready to provide, comfort, and forgive.

These are just some examples of situations that may make us more like Elimelech. Readers may have other life examples of their own, or thoughts and ideas they want to share. Anything that drives us to trust in something other than God for our care and lives is very much like Elimelech's trust in traveling to Moab over his trust in Yahweh to provide.

Regardless the situation, whatever causes to doubt is lamentable. We should repent of our faithless decisions, seek confession and absolution, and rejoice in the faithfulness of God to forgive us through Christ.

3. Despite the ending Elimelech and his sons came to, how does Yahweh show grace and mercy to part of Elimelech's family? When we face difficult times and make mistakes, how does Yahweh show His grace and mercy to us?

Yahweh shows grace and mercy to Naomi by preserving her life despite the deaths of her husband and sons. As the Book of Ruth goes on, it will become clear just how abundant God's grace and mercy is to Naomi, though at this time it seems like it is mostly absent. When we face difficulties and our own sinfulness, we have a sure and certain place to look for Yahweh's grace and mercy for us: we can look to the Means of Grace, those places where Yahweh has promised to be found. These Means of Grace are God's Word and His Sacraments. We find these in the preaching of the Gospel (especially in the assembly of believers), in the proclamation of Absolution, in the waters of Baptism, and in Christ's body and blood in the Lord's Supper. Yahweh can and often does choose to show His grace and mercy in other more subtle ways as well, such as the love of friends, the help of a stranger, or even just our daily sustenance. It is true that Yahweh's grace and mercy is also found in these and many other things, but when there is doubt, or when to all appearances you feel that His grace and mercy are absent for you, there is always one place to look where there is no doubt, and that is to the Means of Grace. In the Divine Service, in private Confession and Absolution with your Pastor, in your Baptism, in the Lord's Supper, in any time someone proclaims the Gospel of Christ crucified for you there you can always know that God in Christ continues to be merciful and gracious to you!

CHAPTER 2:

1. Can we approach God with our laments? What are some examples from Scripture that show us how to plead with God in difficult times?

We can and should approach God with our cares, concerns, and even our grievances against Him. Like Naomi, we can hold God responsible for all that occurs (as He truly is), while at the same time pleading with Him to act according to His gracious will in Christ Jesus. Unlike Naomi, we should not lose hope in Yahweh or His gracious promises, but rather recognize that we must hold Jesus before His eyes and say, "On account of the suffering and death of Your Son, Jesus Christ, on my behalf, be merciful to me in this situation. It is time for You to act according to Your good and gracious will. It is time for relief." It is good to hold God responsible and beg that He act according to His gracious will; it is not right to hold God responsible and as a result turn our backs on Him or turn inward and refuse to see the help He has at hand for us, as did Naomi. While she was right to understand that God should be the one held ultimately responsible for her situation, and while she was right to bring her grievances before Him, she was not right to then ignore the people and situations around her through which Yahweh was already acting (Ruth and the barley harvest).

The Book of Job offers many insights into pleading with God to be merciful as He has promised to be. See Job 19 for one example. Here Job confesses that it is God who has made him wretched, yet he holds God to His promises and also confesses that his Redeemer will come and that, even if Job dies, he will see his Redeemer face-to-face. This is, of course, a confession of Christ. Job has the promise, and he stands in its power.

Jeremiah wrote the Book of Lamentations all about the sorrows that confronted him and his people in the face of God's anger. Take, for example, this section:

> How the Lord in His anger has set the daughter of Zion under a cloud! He has cast down from heaven to earth the splendor of Israel; He has not remembered His footstool in the day of His anger. The Lord has swallowed up without mercy all the inhabitants of Jacob; in His wrath He has broken down the strongholds of the daughter of Judah; He has brought down to the ground in dishonor the kingdom and its rulers. . . . Look, O LORD, and see! With whom have You dealt thus? Should women eat the fruit of their womb, the

children of their tender care? Should priest and prophet be killed in the sanctuary of the Lord? (Lamentations 2:1–2, 20)

Here Jeremiah holds the Lord responsible for the people's misery and directly addresses questions to Yahweh. The answer to the rhetorical questions should be no. These things should not occur, yet they have. Jeremiah brings this and more before Yahweh. Yet, in chapter 3 of Lamentations, Jeremiah confesses that though Yahweh is the one who brought about the calamity, Yahweh is also the one who is faithful and who will finally crush all of Jeremiah's enemies. He confesses that Yahweh has heard his cries for help. Jeremiah says, "You came near when I called on You; You said, 'Do not fear!'" (Lamentations 3:57). Here again, we see a biblical figure addressing his lament to Yahweh, while also confessing that he knows Yahweh will ultimately deliver him according to His grace and mercy. Even when God does not seem to be acting mercifully, these biblical figures hold Him to His gracious promises.

Jesus Himself addresses a lament to Yahweh, asking that the cup pass from Him if possible (Matthew 26:36–46). Yet He does so knowing that, though Yahweh sends Him to His death, He will not leave Him in death. Throughout His life and ministry, Jesus confesses that He will rise from the dead, and Yahweh tells Jesus that He is His beloved Son.

Like Jesus, we have been told we are Yahweh's beloved children, and we have been given His gracious promises through His Son. When we face difficulty, death, or anguish personally or corporately, we can bring our laments to Yahweh, even holding Him to account for them, and we can demand, depend on, and wait for His gracious work to begin.

2. How does the phrase "God is in control" cut both ways with regard to terror and comfort?

Such a phrase is not pure Gospel. It is pure truth, but it is not pure Gospel. Anything that is not pure Gospel can, however well-meant it may be, bring about the Law, rather than the Gospel.

Often, when people say "God is in control," they mean to comfort you. The subtext is, "Your situation looks bad now, but God controls everything, and He'll work it out." While this is true, it is not fully comforting. Yes. God is in control. And famines happen. And fertilizer plants explode. And people bomb marathons. And buildings fall. And parents die. And children die. And jobs are lost. And women are beaten by their husbands. And crops fail. And couples cannot conceive the children they desperately desire. God's control does not sound so comforting in the face of such things. When we are looking at the hidden God being in control, there is no telling what He might do to us fragile, poor, sinful creatures according to His righteousness.

Yes, "God is in control" can also carry with it the idea of His gracious will throughout any difficult circumstance. It can be meant to point the hearer to the time when the present sufferings will make sense in the grand scheme of life, when we can look back and see how God was bringing good out of it (if, indeed, such a time ever does come, which it may not for some situations). Better, though, to speak pure Gospel in pure Gospel ways. Better to acknowledge the situation and its hurtfulness, its gravity, its power, and let the person grieve. When the time is right, then we speak not, "God is in control," but "God in Christ is for you.

God in Christ has died for you and risen for you. God, because of Christ, will raise you up from this dust heap. He will keep His promises to you of life eternal, forgiveness of sins, and resurrection. Come with me to the font and the altar and the pulpit where God in Christ has come to you in the waters of your Baptism, where God in Christ puts the very body and blood of His Son into your mouth to eat and drink, and where God in Christ declares you to be forgiven."

"God is in control" is not bad or wrong. It's just not pure Gospel in pure Gospel words. Let us confess the pure Gospel in Gospel ways instead.

3. How does the narrator help us to peek into God's hidden work behind the scenes in the Book of Ruth?

The narrator does this by addressing the reader directly with certain facts or extra information. The narrator also uses techniques like repetition to help point the reader toward God's gracious activity behind the scenes. For instance, in this chapter, the idea of "turning" is repeatedly used to help us see that Naomi is repentant, but also to remind us that Yahweh Himself has also "repented." He has turned back to His people after years of famine and provides for them again. The verb used for "repent/turn/ return" is also used of Yahweh several times throughout the Old Testament, usually when He is bent on destroying someone for their sins, a faithful servant intercedes, and then Yahweh repents of His intention and "turns" from His wrath to His graciousness. For instance, see Exodus 32:7–14. Here, Yahweh is determined to punish the people after they turn to the golden calf in their idolatry. He says He will make a great nation out of Moses after consuming the Israelites. However, Moses here uses the same verb, nacham, to urge Yahweh to forgive His people. He literally asks Yahweh to "turn" or "repent" from His anger. After Moses' intercessory prayers, Yahweh decides not to bring total disaster upon the Israelites. He turns from His wrath, and instead only about three thousand are punished. By understanding the way this word is used throughout the Old Testament, we can see that the narrator's use of the word points not just to the repentance or turning of people, or just to Naomi's returning home physically, but to how Yahweh is also at work.

Another example of God's hidden work in this chapter is the narrator's focus on two items at the end of the chapter: (1) Ruth's return with Naomi, and (2) the barley harvest. By leaving the main action of the story to remind us of these two key facts, the narrator points toward measures Yahweh already has in store to care for and sustain Ruth and Naomi.

4. Can you think of a time in your life when things looked dark and God seemed distant? To what did you cling during that time? How did God in Christ eventually reveal His gracious self? How might we bring comfort to others in such times? Where should they look?

Answers here may vary. People have had a myriad of experiences we can sometimes not even imagine. For my husband and myself, one such time was when he had graduated with his doctorate in organ performance, but there were no calls for a year's time after his graduation. No one seemed to know what to do with a man who was both a pastor and an organist and had a doctorate. We felt God was very silent for a long time. We held Him to His promises.

This is just an example of a type of response that this question might elicit. If you are working on this book as a group, it is not necessary for everyone or anyone to share personal experiences that they may not be comfortable sharing. However, it can be helpful to bring your cares, concerns, and doubts to fellow Christians. Make sure your group is a safe and confidential space in which that can occur if anyone wishes to share.

It may be possible to share what brought people comfort even without sharing details of the difficulty they faced. Here again, there may be many different answers. For instance, for my husband and I, we held God to His promises, we found comfort in the Divine Service, especially Holy Communion, and we saw God at work through His people in the way in which friends and family cared for us during that time.

When others face difficulties, we should help to care for them as the body of Christ. This may mean taking care of physical and emotional needs as well as spiritual ones. However, no matter how else such comfort takes shape, it should always go hand in hand with the proclamation of the Gospel for that person in her circumstance, and with pointing that person to her Baptism, the Divine Service, Holy Communion, and the preaching of the Gospel as places for her to find comfort and receive God's promised gifts.

5. What did we say was the peak point of this section and why?

    The peak point of this section is, of course, Ruth's confession of Yahweh and her promise to Naomi that Naomi's God will be her God. Ruth's entire speech is a central point, of course, but the central portion of that speech brings Ruth's faithfulness to the forefront. That a Moabite, a pagan woman, promises to follow Naomi's God, Yahweh, and then uses His covenant name while confessing the resurrection of the dead should be shocking and striking, even to our modern selves. Such a confession would not be possible had Yahweh not gifted Ruth with the faith that spoke it.

6. Discuss the return/turn theme of this section. How is that developed throughout the section and what are its theological implications?

    The return/turn theme is developed through the repeated use of the verb turn/return as a leitwort in this section. The verb is used in several different ways. It is used by the narrator to refer to Naomi's return to Israel, and it is used by Naomi in urging her daughters-in-law to return to Moab. The verb both opens and closes the section as it occurs in verses 6 and 22. This use of the verb at both ends of the section creates an inclusio that sets this section of the narrative apart and tells the reader that it has its own important themes and ideas to convey. The peak of this inclusio is, as discussed above, Ruth's confession of Yahweh. The section ends with the narrator again emphasizing Naomi's return to Bethlehem, the fact that Ruth returns with her, and the timing of the return (at the beginning of the barley harvest).

    The leitwort of turn/return reminds us as readers of the repentance that is a part of every Christian's life. Like Naomi, we often must repent or turn back to God from actions or paths that were not of His will. Naomi makes many different kinds of returns here. She returns to her people, her land, and her former town. Her physical return to Bethlehem also signifies a spiritual return. She has at least now, if not before, repented of having turned from

Yahweh to find sustenance elsewhere (in the land of Moab) and is returning to faith in Yahweh's ability to provide. Even if Naomi never fully rejected Yahweh during her years in Moab, her return still signifies repentance of the sin of not fully trusting in His care.

Naomi's return and her repentance also prompt another turning, that of Ruth from her pagan gods to Yahweh. Coming as her speech does at the peak point of the inclusio created by the leitwort, *it becomes clear that the narrator is using this theme of repentance to point to a central idea: that of repentance and faith going hand in hand. When one repents or returns or turns, one turns either from faith to unbelief (as does Orpah in her "return" to "her people" and "her gods") or from unbelief/sin/doubt to belief and faithfulness (as does Ruth). True repentance is prompted by God's gracious activity (Naomi "returns" only after hearing that the Lord has visited His people) and is a result of the faith which that gracious activity creates.*

7. What are some of the ways in both this section and the previous one that the narrator connects Naomi to the matriarchs and patriarchs (i.e., Abraham, Isaac, Rebekah, Leah, Sarah, Rachel, Jacob, etc.) and to the remnant theme?

Naomi and Elimelech are connected to the matriarchs and patriarchs through the event of sojourning. Like the matriarchs and patriarchs of the Genesis accounts, Naomi and Elimelech journey to a foreign land for sustenance during a time of famine. However, as discussed in the chapter, their journey is not the same as those taken by the matriarchs and patriarchs, because the land that had been promised to those figures as a distant reality was now a true reality for Elimelech and Naomi. Yet, Elimelech chooses to turn his back on that promise and leave his land for a pagan country. So while their journey is under similar circumstances, their journey is not one of faithfulness as the journeys of the matriarchs and patriarchs were. Furthermore, Naomi's emptiness, especially with regard to having lost all of her children, is very similar to the barrenness of many of the matriarchs. It is sort of their barrenness in reverse. Rachel, Leah, and Sarah especially struggled with barrenness until Yahweh opened their wombs. Naomi had two children, but she tragically lost them, leaving her almost as bereft of children as a barren woman would be. Furthermore, she laments her current barren state in her inability to have more sons to provide her daughters-in-law with more husbands (referring to Levirate marriage). Since the sons' unions also produced no heirs, the childless state of both Naomi and Ruth is very reminiscent of the barrenness of many of the matriarchs.

The connection to the matriarchs and patriarchs of Genesis is an important one, because it is through them that the promised Seed will be born. In connecting Naomi and Ruth, even subtly at this point, to those Genesis personages, the narrator is hinting at what Yahweh might be doing through them. Though they appear barren currently, will Yahweh work to bring something more through their wombs?

Naomi is also connected to the remnant theme seen most often among the later prophets, such as Isaiah. The remnant is those members of Israel who are still faithful to Yahweh after a period of unfaithfulness or exile, war, famine, or other form of punishment. What is left after these things "winnow away" the unfaithful is the faithful remnant through which Yahweh always continues His gracious activity. Naomi is referred to as being "left" several times in the beginning of Ruth chapter 1. This idea of Naomi being "left," coupled with her use of the name of Yahweh, her prayers for her daughters-in-law, and her return/repentance show us that Naomi is the faithful remnant of this little family that settled in Moab. Ruth can also be seen as part of the remnant here, as she remains with Naomi and also confesses faith in Yahweh.

CHAPTER 3:

1. What are some of the ways in which the narrator has clued us in to Yahweh at work? In what way does the "behind the scenes" work

of Yahweh in Ruth offer comfort to us as Christians today in our own lives?

Throughout the Book of Ruth, the narrator often hints at Yahweh's gracious activity without outright saying "Yahweh did this to be gracious to Naomi and Ruth." He does this in a few different ways. One way in which the narrator hints at Yahweh's gracious activity is by including the blessings and prayers of Yahweh's faithful people. As he records these prayers and blessings, he also records events that fulfill those prayers and blessings, implicitly showing the reader how Yahweh works to answer the prayers of His faithful people. Additionally, the narrator uses narration (as opposed to dialogue) at key junctures to offer clues to the reader. For instance, in chapter 1, he mentions the barley harvest. In chapter 2, he offers some seemingly unrelated information about a relative named Boaz before the main action of the chapter begins. He also uses phrases such as "she happened upon her happenstance" or "and behold!" Such phrases are meant to point the reader to the fact that these events are not accidental, but really a part of God's activity on behalf of Naomi and Ruth.

Understanding that the Lord works to fulfill the prayers of His people, and that He works in often hidden ways, can help us as readers have faith in the work of God on our behalf, even when we cannot see it or understand it. In fact, we may never realize, even in hindsight, all the things God was doing to care for us in our daily lives. By letting us peek behind the veil a bit in the Book of Ruth, the narrator reminds us that God's gracious activity carries on constantly and in all things in order to protect, save, and care for His people.

2. In what ways has Ruth lived according to the spirit, rather than the letter, of the Law? What about Boaz? How does this make them types of Christ?

Ruth technically did not owe her mother-in-law the sacrifice of her own country and her own family. She certainly did not have to go with her to Bethlehem. Yet, Ruth sacrifices all she has ever known and loved to return with Naomi and care for her. Once in Bethlehem, Ruth risks her personal safety by offering to go and glean grain in order to help provide food for them. She does not just glean a little bit of grain or for a small portion of the day, either. She works very hard for the whole day in order to return to her mother-in-law with as much help and comfort as she can. The fact that she has worked very hard is made clear by the foreman when Boaz speaks with him concerning Ruth.

Boaz also acts according to the spirit rather than just the letter of the Law. Rather than just "not murder" Ruth, Boaz cares for Ruth and Naomi in all of their needs (see the discussion in the chapter on the broader interpretation of the Fifth Commandment in Luther's Small Catechism). He also interprets the Law concerning allowing others to glean according to its spirit. He is not stingy with his crops. He allows Ruth to glean in a more advantageous position and even has his bundlers leave out handfuls of grain for her to find. Keep in mind that Boaz's generosity with his crops also follows on years of famine. If at any time it would have been understandable for the Israelites to be protective of where their crops went, it would be at the first harvest after a long famine. However, Boaz is almost recklessly generous to Ruth and Naomi.

In interpreting the Law according to its spirit rather than just its letter, both Ruth and Boaz are types of Christ. First of all, it is Christ Himself who fulfilled the Law by going above and beyond it. Jesus does not just feed those who are hungry, He feeds them until they are satisfied and have an abundance left over (think of the feeding of the five thousand). He does not just care for their physical hunger and thirst, but their spiritual hunger and thirst as well. He feeds them on His Word, and ultimately, on His own body and blood. Jesus does not just "not murder" His neighbor; He actually raises His neighbor from the dead (e.g., Jairus's daughter, the widow's son, Lazarus) and promises to do

185

the same for all of us. In all that He is and does, Jesus fulfills the Law and goes beyond its requirements to fulfill not only the letter, but also the spirit of the Law.

3. When thinking through the different type-scenes and Jesus' life, can you pinpoint the events in Jesus' life that fulfill some of these scenes?

A few that will most likely be the quickest to come to mind are:

Annunciation: *Gabriel's announcement to Mary that she will conceive and bear a son (Luke 1).*

Initiatory Trial/Danger and Discovery of Sustenance in the Wilderness: *Jesus' temptation, which is His initial test and after which His ministry begins, and the subsequent care given to Him by the angels who ministered to Him (see Matthew 4:1–11).*

Testament of the Dying Hero: *The Lord's Supper, Jesus' new testament in His blood shed for the life of the world.*

CHAPTER 4:

1. Ruth's garments of widowhood and the Israelites' traditions for periods of mourning indicate to others, even strangers, that she is mourning. It also gives her a marked time period to publicly grieve. Often, this period was at least one year long. How do we mark our losses in our society today? How is it sufficient or insufficient? Do you think there might have been something helpful about the traditions of the Israelites? What are some ways that, even without garments of mourning to remind us, we can enter into the grieving of our friends and remember their losses over an extended period of time?

Answers here might vary a bit, and that is fine, as some of these questions are really about people's opinions or feelings. However, the ultimate goal of this question will be to redirect the discussion toward how Yahweh is with us in our grief, as well as ways in which we can remember others in their grief. Here are some sample thoughts to get you going.

The helpful thing about the Israelite tradition is that it not only allows others to understand that you are still in a period of grieving, but it allows the person who is grieving to do so without shame or feeling as if he/she should "get over it" or "move on." Sometimes, in our society, after the funeral there is not much recognition of a person's loss beyond a few months. Often people feel pressured, if not explicitly then at least implicitly, to move past their grief fairly quickly and cover it up even sooner. They are expected to jump back into work and life quickly and without any significant change in their behavior. The attention and care of others often tapers off long before the grief begins to even become just a little less intense. Funerals are wonderful, helpful, important steps in the grieving process. A good funeral should proclaim Christ crucified for not only the deceased, but all those in attendance. It should put hope in the resurrection of the dead and in God's gift of Baptism. However, the grieving lasts much longer than that. Sometimes the shock does not wear off until at least a year later. Then there is the process of finding out who you are now that you are defining yourself as a person without a particular parent, or without any parents, or without a spouse, or without a child. We don't have to reinstitute garments of widowhood here, but there are ways that we can help and support those who grieve among us. Here are just a few thoughts:

◇ Proclaim the Gospel of Christ crucified and resurrected to the person.

◇ Ask if they need anything, but remember that not everyone is comfortable with admitting they need help. So if you see a need, go ahead and find a way to fill it.

◇ Reach out to them in mercy through organizing meals for several weeks after the death.

◇ Phone them once or twice a week for a few months afterward, just to chat or check in.

◇ After a few months, if you can, go out to see a movie or out to dinner.

- *For a widow, have an adult girls' night sleepover with wine, cheese, cake, and such after some time has passed.*

- *For a widower or grieving man, talk with your husband, brother, or another male friend about his comfort level in joining that person in their favorite activity or having dinner.*

- *Have them over for dinner . . . get them out of their house.*

- *Point the person to Yahweh's promises of comfort and His promise to wipe away every tear (see Revelation 21:4).*

- *Point the person to Yahweh's continued care of him or her through friends, family, and the Church. Direct him or her most especially to the proclamation of the Gospel, the Lord's Supper, and his or her Baptism.*

- *Send occasional cards, care packages, or little notes if you are far away. Handwritten is better.*

- *Remind the person of Yahweh's gracious acts towards their loved one.*

- *Remember significant anniversaries, such as the one year anniversary of the person's death, the first holiday after the person's death, and the loved one's birthday. For the loss of a spouse, note the anniversary. Give the person a call or a card on these days, or make plans with them.*

- *For a miscarriage or stillbirth, recall the due date, when the child's first birthday would have been, the time of the year when the couple conceived, and even smaller milestones like when the child would have turned one month or six months old. Holidays when the child would have first been present with the family will also be extremely difficult.*

Yahweh was demonstrably with Ruth and Naomi through those who cared for them and through His provision of food. He was with Naomi through Ruth, who cared for her in her grief beyond what was even expected. Yahweh is also with us when we grieve through His Divine Service to us and through the love and care of friends and family. But even when friends and family fall away or forget or get busy with their own lives (and even when we do this to those in our lives who grieve), Yahweh always remains.

2. Think of a time when you have been empty and Yahweh has filled you. In what way were you empty? How did He fill you? How does He fill us each and every Sunday?

Again, answers here will obviously vary. A time in my life when I felt very empty, for example, was when I had finished my freshman year at the University of Iowa. My family's finances were low, and the financial aid was not as much as we needed to make returning for my sophomore year affordable. I felt horrible. I thought I might have to return home and think of some other plan for my education. I had found a wonderful church home at the LCMS Campus Ministry in Iowa City (St. Paul Lutheran Chapel and University Center), and I loved the academic opportunities I had at the university. It really looked as if I would not be going back. I could not understand why God would put me at Iowa in the first place, lead me to the LCMS through the Campus Ministry, and then cut my time there so short. However, after writing a letter to the financial aid office, praying, and watching, the Lord provided more funds so that I could return to the university. My pastor said to me, "Sometimes the Lord has to bring you all the way down so He can pick you back up." Another way of saying that would be to say that sometimes Yahweh has to empty you out to fill you up. Sometimes He has to bring you to the depths of despair before He can raise you to thankfulness and praise. Sometimes He has to kill you to make you alive.

Which brings us to how Yahweh fills us every Sunday. In our Baptisms, Yahweh kills us to make us alive. We die to sin, death, and the devil, we die to self, and we rise to righteousness, bless-

edness, life, and forgiveness. Every Sunday, we are reminded of our Baptisms, where we were emptied of self and filled with the faith that clings to Christ when the pastor speaks God's triune name and we make the sign of the cross. In the pastor's preaching, Yahweh fills us up with His life-giving Word. In the Lord's Supper, Yahweh fills our empty vessels with the very body and blood of our Lord Jesus Christ, which brings life, healing, comfort, joy, peace, and forgiveness. In the Lord's Supper, we are connected to all the fellow Christians communing with us, and to the communion of saints and all the company of heaven, as we confess in the Proper Preface. We are filled, then, with the love and support of fellow Christians in time and in eternity. What a wonderful blessing to know that all of our fellow Christians share our burdens and our joys when we commune together at the altar! It is through these things that Yahweh brings fullness in our emptiness, in every kind of emptiness. Even physical emptiness is filled here as we can seek the help and support of our fellow Christians for the needs of daily life.

We have often found, though, that we need not seek it out at all. The generosity of God's people is indeed like that of their Savior, for they are being conformed to His image daily. Prompted by the gifts of their Lord, they often give generously to those in their midst whom they know to be struggling, even without being asked. We have experienced this generosity again and again as a family during my husband's years earning his higher education degrees while working part-time as a pastor, and during our time gathering the funds needed to deploy as missionaries to Germany. Trust in Yahweh's graciousness through His Means of Grace and through His people, your family in Christ.

3. If someone asked you, "Where is Yahweh in the Book of Ruth?" how would you answer them so far?

   One key way we can see Yahweh at work is in the prayers and blessings pronounced throughout Ruth so far. Some of them have already been answered in full or in part. Plus, any time the name of Yahweh is used, it means that Yahweh is at work in that person, for no one can confess Yahweh without the work of the Holy Spirit.

Additionally, Yahweh is at work through His provision of Ruth to Naomi. Through Ruth, He ministers to Naomi both spiritually and physically.

Yahweh is at work through the barley harvest to provide for the physical needs of both Ruth and Naomi, as well as all of His people. As Naomi confesses in chapter 1, it is Yahweh who has visited the fields to give them yield.

4. Is Boaz, as the "redeemer" of Naomi and Ruth, also a type of Christ? What characteristics or actions of Boaz point forward to Christ so far in the Book of Ruth?

Yes. Boaz is very much a type of Christ in the Book of Ruth. This becomes clear especially in chapters 3 and 4, but is also evidenced earlier. Boaz provides for Ruth and Naomi physically through his generosity in giving a portion of his harvest to them. His gifts of barley go above and beyond what the Law requires when he allows Ruth to glean so closely behind his own reapers. He also gives her more than the Law requires when he invites her to dine with his workers and himself. Furthermore, Boaz demonstrates that, like Christ, he is willing to sacrifice for the sake of others in that giving so much of his harvest for free to Ruth and Naomi is a sacrifice of income. This is especially striking due to the fact that this is apparently the first year that sustenance and profit have been possible due to the famine. Boaz's faithfulness to Yahweh also contributes to how he is emerging as a type of Christ in these final chapters. Boaz's greetings to his workers and his prayers and blessings of Ruth show that he is faithful to Yahweh and trusts in Him.

5. If you had to pinpoint a strong theological theme in this section based on the text, themes with which you are familiar, and our

discussion, what would it be? What does it tell us about Yahweh?

The strongest theme in this chapter is probably redemption, as it is stressed by the leitwort. *The theme of redemption in this section refers forward to the redemption that Yahweh will accomplish for all of His people. It also includes the individual and mini-redemptions God consistently brings about for the life of the world and the sake of those whom He loves. For instance, God redeemed His people from slavery in Egypt. He bought them back by way of His miraculous acts. He is working in the Book of Ruth to buy back Ruth and Naomi's land through Boaz, His servant. The emphasis on redemption in this chapter reminds the hearers and the readers that redemption is Yahweh's work. He prefers to do the work of redeeming—in other words, Yahweh prefers to act according to His grace and mercy, rather than His wrath. All that He does in the Old Testament leads up to His final redemption of all people.*

The other themes discussed in this chapter would also be great for further discussion, but probably are not as strong as the theme of redemption.

CHAPTER 5:

1. How do we find a connection between Ruth and Proverbs 31:10–31? List some of the clues given to us by the texts, the narrator, and the compilers of the Hebrew canon.

    The texts of the Book of Ruth and Proverbs 31 bear similarities in both characteristics and linguistics. The Hebrew word for "worthy" or "strength" is used of both Ruth and the woman of Proverbs 31. Both women work hard for their families in a self-initiated and self-sacrificial manner. Additionally, both women fear Yahweh. It is Ruth's faithfulness to Yahweh and to Naomi that garners her praise (Boaz tells her in chapter 2 that he has heard of all she has done for Naomi), and it is the loving care and faithfulness displayed by the woman of Proverbs 31 that lead to her being praised "in the gates." The narrator uses the word wor-

thy *of both Ruth and Boaz, flagging this as an important concept in the Book of Ruth. This leads the reader to pay attention to its use and meaning, as well as other places where it can be found.*

The compilers of the original Hebrew canon placed Ruth after Proverbs 31:10–31 among the Writings. They did so despite the fact that Ruth is chronologically related to the Book of Judges. It seems the compilers saw the connection between Ruth and the woman of Proverbs 31. While Proverbs 31 describes the woman who fears the Lord, the woman of "worth" or "strength," the Book of Ruth offers an example of a real woman who fit this description.

2. What are some of the linguistic and subject similarities between Proverbs 8 and Proverbs 31 discussed in this chapter?

This question can be easily discussed by referring back to the chart in chapter 5 of this book. Linguistically speaking, there are many words and phrases that are either identical or similar, such as "the fear of the LORD," "fruit," "kindness," and "in the gates." All of these also contribute to subject similarities between the two chapters of Proverbs, including the idea that both speak well and with wisdom, both are active and not idle, both are wise, and both offer what is better than fine gold, silver, or jewels. These are just a few of the similarities. These similarities help us to understand that the speaker of Proverbs 8, Lady Wisdom, is the woman of Proverbs 31:10–31.

3. Discuss the difference between a prescriptive text and a descriptive text. How is Proverbs 31 often treated—as prescriptive or as descriptive? How should it be understood?

A prescriptive text instructs the reader or hearer to do or not do a particular thing. A prescriptive text gives direction for life and faith; it is meant to be followed. The Ten Commandments are an easily recognizable prescriptive text. These are texts that we are meant to follow and do. A descriptive text describes an event or sometimes relates a custom in the history of God's people. The event or custom is not prescriptive of how we should act or what we should subscribe to today. A good example of this is 1 Corinthians 11:2–16, where Paul discusses head coverings. Many people over time have believed that this means a woman must wear a head covering of some sort (in American culture, usually a hat) in order to comply with the way in which God would have women dress. The head coverings in this chapter refer to what at that time was proper dress for a married woman. This was a way in which people could see that a woman was married and not an unmarried maiden. To take the head covering off could be interpreted as a sign of availability. This text describes a practice at the time that for us can offer a principle. For instance, we might liken this to a married woman today entering a bar, slipping off her wedding ring, and then presenting herself as available to the males in the bar, or if not doing so intentionally, at least causing confusion by her actions and the absence of her wedding ring. Paul is pointing to the root of this issue: the man is the head of the woman, Christ is the head of the man, and God is the head of Christ. There is a certain order to all things. The order that God has intended should be respected and embraced. So while this text teaches us about God's order and the fact that it should be respected, the detail of the head covering is not a prescriptive instruction for all women of all time to cover their heads, but an example of the way in which they showed their respect for God's given order in that time.

Proverbs 31 is often taken as a prescriptive text. It can be used to tell women how they should be and act, and everything that they should do. This might be done for good or bad intentions. Some might use it to order women to do all these things. Sometimes, though, well-meaning women's ministries or devotions might use this text to tell women what they should do to be godly women. They do not mean to hurt or subjugate women, but by not understanding how this text taken prescriptively puts the yoke of the Law upon women, they do a disservice. Proverbs 31:10–31 is descriptive of the woman who fears the Lord, who is Wisdom, who is ultimately Jesus. From it we can draw hope and comfort

*in knowing that because Jesus is Wisdom, He already does all of
these things in and through us. So instead of striving to become
the woman of Proverbs 31, we can rest assured in the fact that,
because we are in Christ, we already are the worthy woman who
fears the Lord.*

4. Similarly, is Ruth sometimes treated as a prescription for how we
    should act? How does our perception of Ruth and of how Ruth
    speaks to us today change if we understand her and her history as
    descriptive?

    *Ruth, like the woman of Proverbs 31, is often upheld as a good
    example of "how to be a godly woman." Questions about the
    Book of Ruth might tend to center on what Ruth can teach us
    about what to do in order to be labeled a godly woman, or on the
    idea that we should live out our lives exactly like Ruth did by
    sacrificing ourselves in the same way she did, or something simi-
    lar. Besides the fact that this is a slightly absurd idea, since Ruth
    lived thousands of years ago, in a different time, and in very
    different circumstances than ours, it tends to throw the focus on
    what we can do and on Ruth's deeds more than on what God has
    done through Ruth. To be sure, it is good to have good examples
    of faithful women, and there are things we can learn from them.
    However, the main focus should not be on how to "be more like
    Ruth." It should be on how Ruth's history points us to Jesus. By
    understanding Ruth's story mainly as descriptive of Yahweh and
    His working through particular people in a particular time for
    particular reasons, the Book of Ruth becomes not a prescrip-
    tion for better living, but a proclamation of the Gospel for us.*

CHAPTER 6:

1. Discuss the inclusio formed by Ruth 1:5 and 4:16. How has the
    narrative come full circle? How did the intervening events all work
    to bring these two verses together?

    *The inclusio is formed by similar words in 1:5 and 4:16. The
    word in Hebrew is the word for young boys, and can usually be*

understood more as "boys." This would not have been used of men of Mahlon and Chilion's age, yet the narrator uses it in 1:5 to refer to Naomi's sons after they die. The sense is that she is left without her little boys. In 4:16, the same word is used of Obed as he is laid in Naomi's lap as an infant. It is often translated here as "child," but is the same word meaning a young boy. Within this inclusio, things come full circle for Naomi. All of the events of the intervening verses stem from this moment of loss to the moment of fullness when Obed is laid in Naomi's lap. The journey back to Bethlehem, Ruth's speech of faith, the barley and wheat harvests, Boaz's help and generosity, Naomi's plan, Ruth's visit to the threshing floor, the transaction at the town gate, and the marriage of Boaz and Ruth with the resulting conception and birth of Obed all culminate in the moment when Naomi, bereft of her "little boys," once again takes a "little boy" in her arms. God uses all that occurs in between to bring Naomi from emptiness to fullness and from bitter to pleasant. The inclusio highlights how God works through seemingly ordinary things like human decisions on the part of Naomi, Ruth, and Boaz; harvests and gleaning; laws concerning kinsman-redeemers; practices such as Levirate marriage; and the prayers and blessings people speak. All of these things worked together to bring Naomi back to where she started, in a sense, but even better. For she not only has been filled with her "little boy" Obed, but she has returned home, symbolizing her return to Yahweh. She has regained the land that was her husband's, and she has the comfort of both Ruth and Obed in her old age.

2. Whose actions are the main focus of the first part of chapter 4 (vv.1–12)? How does this shift in focus, as well as everything we know about him, show us that Boaz is a type of Christ?

    Throughout the first three chapters, the actions of Ruth and Naomi form a center portion of the narrative. Ruth especially comes to the forefront in these chapters in her loving service to Naomi. Ruth, as we have previously shown, is a type of Christ.

Now, in chapter 4, the main action shifts to Boaz. Ruth and Naomi now become the object of the actions of Boaz, the subject.

The shift in focus helps us to now focus on Boaz and, in so doing, highlights his Christlike characteristics and actions. The narrator has previously called Boaz "worthy." This is the same word used of Ruth, and of the woman of Proverbs 31:10–31, and of Lady Wisdom in Proverbs 8. The word itself connects Boaz also to the type of worthiness shown by these other instances. This means that he is faithful and works hard to care for his neighbors, both family and non-family. This idea that Boaz is worthy is introduced in the first few verses of chapter 2 of the Book of Ruth and is then shown to be true by the descriptions of Boaz's words and actions that follow. Boaz greets his workers in the name of Yahweh, showing his faithfulness to Yahweh. He shows overwhelming generosity to Ruth by going above and beyond the Law in providing for a foreigner, which was not required, and by providing more grain than was required, even to the point of having his bundlers purposefully leave out handfuls for Ruth. Boaz's generosity and his adherence not just to the letter, but to the spirit of the Law point forward to Jesus' keeping of the whole Law for us.

Also, Boaz is a kinsman-redeemer. As such, he sacrifices his own interests in order to rescue Ruth and Naomi by buying back their land. Yahweh is the Kinsman-Redeemer who is greater than all human kinsman-redeemers. He sends His very own Son as the price for our sins, in order to buy us back from slavery to sin, death, and the devil, and restore us to life and to our inheritance of eternal life. Jesus can also be seen as our Kinsman-Redeemer. He gives Himself as the price for our rescue. Since Jesus is God, this can be seen both ways. Boaz is, then, a type of Christ. He gives us a picture of all that Christ will be and do for us (though Boaz is, of course, not perfect and does not have every characteristic of Christ).

3. How does the narrator use the nearer redeemer in relation to Boaz?

   The narrator uses the nearer redeemer as a foil for Boaz. By including the nearer redeemer and showing us his shortcomings, the narrator highlights again Boaz's strengths and Christlike characteristics. The nearer redeemer is selfish, uncertain, uncaring, and not even worth naming. He brings on himself the punishment of his name being not even remembered in Israel (and thereby completely dishonored) when he draws off his sandal to complete the transaction. Boaz, on the other hand, has his name renowned in all Israel because of his self-sacrificial generosity and loving-kindness (chesed). Boaz is very sure in his care and concern for Ruth and Naomi and very purposeful in carrying out his intentions to help them.

4. What characteristics or circumstances of Obed make him a type of Christ, as well?

   ◇ *Obed's conception is given by Yahweh—Jesus' conception is given by God to the Virgin Mary.*

   ◇ *Obed comes as a baby to be a redeemer for Naomi and Ruth—Jesus comes as a baby to be the redeemer of the whole world.*

   ◇ *Obed's name means "servant" or "worshiper"— Jesus is the greatest servant and worshiper of God.*

   ◇ *Obed's name is renowned throughout Israel— Jesus' name is renowned throughout Israel, the world, and all time.*

   ◇ *Obed resurrects Elimelech's family— Jesus is the resurrection and the life.*

CHAPTER 7:

1. Here is a chart showing all of the blessings in the Book of Ruth. Find each blessing and then complete the chart by briefly showing how it is fulfilled either within the Book of Ruth, beyond the Book of Ruth, and/or in Jesus.

Blessing	Fulfillment in Ruth	Fulfillment beyond Ruth	Fulfillment in Jesus
Ruth 1:8–9	*Ruth's marriage to Boaz and the birth of Obed.*	*Rest and security in her home with Boaz until her death; rest and security as a member of Yahweh's people.*	*Eternal rest in Jesus; Jesus is Ruth's rest.*
Ruth 2:4	*Boaz's good harvest, marriage to Ruth, and a son being born to him through her.*	*Boaz is blessed as a member of Yahweh's people for all of time.*	*Ultimately, Boaz and all people are fully and eternally blessed through Jesus Christ.*
Ruth 2:12	*Ruth is repaid and given a reward from Yahweh when she marries Boaz and bears Obed.*	*Another part of Ruth's reward is her becoming the ancestress of King David.*	*Ultimately, Ruth's reward is Jesus Christ for her life, forgiveness, and salvation.*
Ruth 2:19	*Again, Boaz is blessed by Yahweh in numerous ways in the conclusion of the book: a good harvest, Ruth as a wife, and a son, Obed.*	*Again, the fulfillment of this one is basically the same as in 2:4. Boaz is blessed with the covenantal promises of Yahweh.*	*Again, Boaz and all people are blessed by God in Christ for us.*
Ruth 3:10	*Boaz himself fulfills his own prayer for Ruth by being a blessing to her in becoming her Levir and redeemer.*	*Continued blessings in their lives together, the blessing of a future king from their line, etc.*	*Again, Yahweh blesses Ruth by making her a part of His covenant people and even a part of the lineage of Jesus.*

Ruth 4:11–12	The birth of Obed fulfills the prayer for Ruth to build up the house of Boaz, Boaz has already acted worthily, and his name is renowned.	Beyond the Book of Ruth, the prayer to build up Boaz's house is fulfilled in the birth of King David. Through David, Boaz's name is even more renowned as an ancestor of the king.	The prayer for Boaz's house to be built up is finally fulfilled in Jesus Christ, to whom this line and "house" has been pointing all along. Boaz's name achieves even more renown as an ancestor of Jesus, and in the fact that Jesus' is the most renowned and honored name in all history.
Ruth 4:14–15	This blessing for Naomi is first fulfilled in the communal naming of Obed, whose name is thereby "renowned" from his very birth.	Obed's name is further renowned as an ancestor of King David.	Obed's name is finally renowned as an ancestor of Jesus.

2. How is the genealogy a fitting capstone for the Book of Ruth?

    The genealogy is a fitting ending to the Book of Ruth for two reasons. First, the genealogy helps to further solidify one of the narrator's purposes. That purpose was to show that David was worthy of being king. The genealogy connects David to an important Old Testament family line to show that he comes from worthy and important ancestors in Israel's past.

    Secondly, the genealogy serves as a connection between Ruth and the matriarchs and patriarchs to whom the original promise was given. This shows the continuity in how and why Yahweh works to bring about His promises.

    In terms of the literary structure, the genealogy serves as an epilogue that completes the prologue function of verses 1 through 5 of chapter 1. It takes the narrative from complete emptiness to complete fullness in showing how the line continues to extend to King David.

3. How does the genealogy point us forward to David and then to Christ?

    The genealogy makes a connection between the matriarchs and King David by showing how the line moves from Perez to David through the birth of Obed to Boaz and Ruth. This demonstrates how Yahweh is working to bring about His purposes in anointing David as King of Israel.

    Finally, in conjunction with Matthew's continuation of it, the genealogy connects us to Jesus Christ. Jesus is both David's Son and David's Lord. The genealogy shows how He is the Son of David by virtue of His human ancestry since He was born of a woman.

4. What are the different ways in which the Book of Ruth has shown us Jesus in some way?

    The Book of Ruth has shown us Jesus through Ruth and Boaz's functions as types of Christ. As types of Christ, both Boaz and Ruth demonstrate characteristics of Jesus: they go above and beyond the requirements of the Law, they serve their neighbor, and they are self-sacrificial. Obed, as a baby who is born in order to redeem Ruth and Naomi, is also a type of Jesus, the baby who is born to redeem the world. The prayers of the Book of Ruth show us Jesus as well in how He fulfills those prayers. The focus on Yahweh's chesed *shows us Jesus because He is the ultimate expression and fulfillment of that* chesed. *He is the one who brings Yahweh's* chesed *to us. Finally, Jesus comes clear through the genealogy and its connection with the genealogy in the Book of Matthew.*

    In all the ways that Ruth shows us Jesus, it shows us Jesus for us. Ruth is a love story from Yahweh to His people.

APPENDIX B:

Author's Translation of the Book of Ruth

TRANSLATION OF CHAPTER 1

1: And it took place in the days the judges were judging that there was a famine in the land and a man went out from Bethlehem of Judah to sojourn in the fields of Moab; he and his wife and his two sons.

2: And the name of the man was Elimelech and the name of his wife was Naomi and the names of his two sons were Mahlon and Chilion, they were Ephrathites from Bethlehem of Judah. And they went to the fields of Moab and they lived there.

3: And when Elimelech, the husband of Naomi, died, she and her two sons were left.

4: And they took for themselves Moabite wives; the name of one was Orpah and the name of the other was Ruth and they dwelt there about ten years.

5: Then both[57] Mahlon and Chilion died so that she was left without her two sons and her husband.

6: And she and her daughters-in-law arose and returned from the fields of Moab, for she had heard in the fields of Moab that Yahweh had visited his people to give them bread.

7: And she went out from the place[58] where she lived and her two daughters-in-law with her and they walked in the road to return to the land of Judah.

8: But Naomi said to her two daughters-in-law, "Go, return each to your mother's household. May Yahweh practice faithfulness with you as you have done to the dead and to me.

---

57   The Hebrew word used here serves to intensify, and in conjunction with the following plural of the word for "two," as well as the listing of both of the their names, greatly intensifes and emphasizes the loss sustained by Naomi.

58   Wilch, 132: This phrase is reminiscent of the exodus from Egypt (Exodus 13:3, Deuteronomy 4:45–46). Also of the promise of a future exodus which is fulfilled in Christ.

9: May Yahweh grant to you that you find a resting place [security: Wilch, 134], each one, in the house of her husband." Then she kissed them and they lifted up their voices as they wailed.

10: But they said to her, "No, we will return with you."

11: But Naomi said, "Return, my daughters. Why do you go with me? [Are there] still for me sons in my womb that they would be for you husbands?

12: Return my daughters, go, for I am old to have a husband; I say if one existed for me, would you indeed wait if I had this very night a man and indeed if I bore sons?

13: Therefore would you wait until when they were grown? Therefore would you keep withdrawn to have no husband? No, my daughters, for it is very bitter for me, for your sakes, that the hand of Yahweh has gone out against me.[59]"

14: Then they lifted up their voices and wept again and Orpah kissed her mother-in-law, but Ruth clung to her.

15: Then she said, "Behold, your sister-in-law has returned to her people and to her gods; return with your sister-in-law."

16: But Ruth said, "Do not urge me to forsake you or to turn from following you; for to where you go, I will go; and where you live, I will live; your people, my people; and your God, my God.

17: Where you die, I will die and there I will be buried, thus may Yahweh grant to me, and thus even death will not separate me from you."

18: When she perceived that she persisted in walking with her, she let her continue on the road with her.

19: And the two walked until she arrived in Bethlehem and it happened when they arrived in Bethlehem that the whole city was in an uproar on account of them and these ones spoke to Naomi.

20: But she said to them, "Do not call me Naomi; call me Mara (bitter), for the hand of the Almighty has gone against me.

---

59   Note significance of this phrase and what the "Hand of Yahweh" can do.

21: I left full, but empty[60] has Yahweh brought me back. Why do you call me Naomi when Yahweh has testified against me and the Almighty has afflicted me?"

22: So Naomi returned and Ruth, the Moabitess, her daughter-in-law, with her returned from the fields of Moab and they arrived in Bethlehem in the beginning of the barley harvest.

TRANSLATION OF CHAPTER 2

1: Now there was to Naomi a kinsman of her husband, a man of great worth[61] from the clan of Elimelech, and his name was Boaz.

2: Then Ruth the Moabitess said to Naomi, "Please let me go to the field and let me glean among the ears of grain behind one in whose eyes I find favor." And Naomi said, "Go, my daughter."

3: And she went and she arrived and she gleaned in a field behind the reapers and she happened to come upon the plot of field belonging to Boaz, who was of the clan of Elimelech.

4: And behold! Boaz came from Bethlehem and said to the reapers, "Yahweh be with you," and they said to him, "Yahweh bless you!"

5: Then Boaz said to his servant, the foreman over the reapers, "Whose is this young woman?"

6: And the servant, the foreman over the reapers, answered and said, "It is a young Moabitess, she returned with Naomi from the region of Moab.

7: And she said, 'Let me glean and gather among the sheaves behind the reapers,' and she went and stayed from the morning until now, this one sitting in the house a little."

8: Then Boaz said to Ruth, "Do you not hear, my daughter? Do not go to glean in another field and indeed do not cross over from this one, but instead stay close with my young women.

9: Put your eyes on the field which they reap and go behind them.

---

60 The word here is that specifically meaning "without property and without family." It is related to the word simply for "empty," but is more specific in the type of emptiness.

61 This word can also mean wealth or strength. Although Boaz is possibly wealthy, "honor" or "worth" better conveys both his character and his standing in the town. Also, this word will later be used of Ruth and to show the connection between the two and their similar characteristics, it is best to translate this as "worth."

Did I not order the young men not to touch you? And if you thirst, go to the vessels and drink of that which the young men draw."

10: Then she fell upon her face and bowed to the ground and said to him, "Why do I find favor in your eyes that you show consideration to me when I am a foreigner?"

11: And Boaz answered and said to her, "It has been fully reported[62] to me all that you did for your mother-in-law after the death of your husband and how you left your father and your mother and the land of your birth and came to a people you did not know until now.

12: May Yahweh reward your work and may there be a full reward from Yahweh, the God of Israel, under whose wings you came to seek refuge."

13: Then she said, "Let me find favor in your eyes, Lord, for you comforted me and spoke kindly to your handmaiden, though I am not one of your handmaidens."

14: And Boaz said to her, when it was time for eating, "Come here and eat of the bread and dip your piece in the vinegar." Then she sat beside the reapers and he passed to her the parched grain and she ate and was satisfied, and she had some left over.

15: When she arose to glean, Boaz ordered his young men saying, "Allow her to glean even among the sheaves and do not hinder her.

16: Even be sure to pull out [some] for her from the bundles of grain and leave [them] behind so that she will glean; and do not rebuke her."

17: She gleaned in the field until the evening, then she beat out what she had gleaned and it was about an ephah of barley.

18: Then she lifted it up and entered the city and her mother-in-law saw what she had gleaned and set forth and gave to her which she had left over after she was satisfied.

19: Then her mother-in-law said to her, "Where did you glean today and where did you work? Blessed be the one who showed you favor." Then she told her mother-in-law with whom she had worked

---

62   An instance of Hebrew intensification—the same verb for "report" is here used in both the infinitive absolute and the third perfect to show that it has really all been told.

and she said, "The name of the man with whom I worked today is Boaz."

20: Then Naomi said to her daughter-in-law, "Blessed be he by Yahweh, who has not forsaken His faithfulness to the living and the dead!" And Naomi said to her, "The man is near to us, he is one of our redeemers.

21: Then Ruth the Moabitess said, "He also said to me, 'Cling with my young women until they have finished all of my harvest.'"

22: Then Naomi said to Ruth, her daughter-in-law, "It is good, my daughter, that you go out with his young women so that they do not attack you in another field."

23: So she clung to Boaz's young women to glean until the end of the barley harvest and the wheat harvest and she lived with her mother-in-law.

TRANSLATION OF CHAPTER 3

1: Then Naomi, her mother-in-law, said to her, "My daughter, should not I seek for you security (rest) so that it may go well for you?

2: And now, is not Boaz our kinsman with whose maidens you were? Behold, he is winnowing at the threshing floor the barley harvest tonight.

3: Therefore wash and anoint [yourself] and put on your mantle upon yourself, then go down to the threshing floor. Do not make yourself known to the man until he has finished eating and drinking.

4: Let it be that when he lies down you will note the place where he lies and go and uncover his feet and lie down and he will tell you what to do."

5: Then she said to her, "All you have said to me, I will do."

6: Then she went down to the threshing floor and did all that her mother-in-law had commanded her.

7: When Boaz had eaten and drunk and his heart was well pleased, then he went to lie down at the edge of a heap of wheat. Then she went softly and uncovered his feet and lay down.

8: It was the middle of the night when the man shuddered and felt around and behold, a woman was lying at his feet.

9: And he said, "Who are you?" And she said, "I am Ruth, your handmaiden; now spread your wing[63] upon your handmaiden for you are a redeemer."

10: Then he said to her, "Blessed are you by the Lord, my daughter; you have showed your faithfulness more now than at the beginning by not following after the young men, whether poor or rich.

11: But now, my daughter, do not fear; all that you have said, I will do for you for all of my people at the gate know that you are an honorable woman.

12: Now, it is true that I am a redeemer, but there is a redeemer even closer than I.

13: Remain through the night and when it is morning, if he will redeem you, good, let him redeem you; but if he is not willing to redeem you, then I myself will redeem you, by Yahweh! Lie down until the morning.

14: So she lay down at his feet until the morning and she arose before a man would recognize his friend because he said, "Let no one know that the woman came to the threshing floor."

15: Then he said, "Give to me the mantle which is upon you and hold it out." And she held it out and he measured out six [measures] of barley and laid [them] upon it. Then he went into the city.

16: Then she went to her mother-in-law and she said to her, "What has happened to you, my daughter?" Then she told her all that the man had done for her.

17: And she said, "These six [measures] of barley he gave to me, for he said, 'Do not go empty to your mother-in-law.'"

18: Then she said to her, "Sit, my daughter, until you know how the matter will turn out; for he will not be idle until he has finished the matter today."

---

63 This is the same Hebrew word that Boaz uses in his prayer in 2:12 when he prays that Ruth may find refuge under Yahweh's wings.

TRANSLATION OF CHAPTER 4

1: Then Boaz went up to the gate and sat there and behold, the redeemer crossed by, of whom Boaz had spoken, and he said, "Turn aside, sit here so-and-so," and he turned aside and sat.

2: And he took ten men from the elders of the city and he said, "Sit here," and they sat.

3: And he said to the redeemer, "A piece of land which belonged to our brother Elimelech, Naomi wishes to sell, the one having returned from the region of Moab.

4: For I thought, 'I will publish it in your ears, saying, Acquire it, tell all those sitting and tell to the elders of my people if you will indeed redeem, but if you will not redeem, let me know, then I will know, for there is no one beside you to redeem, but I myself am after you.'" Then he said, "I will redeem."

5: Then Boaz said, "The day when you acquire for yourself the field from the hand of Naomi I will acquire Ruth, the Moabitess, the wife of the deceased, in order to raise up the name of the deceased in his inheritance."

6: Then the redeemer said, "I am not able to redeem [it] for myself, lest I ruin my inheritance. You redeem for yourself my right of redemption, or I am not able to redeem it."

7: Now this was [the custom] formerly in Israel concerning redemption and concerning exchanging: to confirm the whole matter, a man would take off his sandal and give it to his friend and this was attestation in Israel.

8: Then the redeemer said to Boaz, "Acquire [it] for yourself"; and he took off his sandal.

9: Then Boaz said to the elders and all the people, "You are witnesses today that I have acquired all which belonged to Elimelech and all which belonged to Chilion and Mahlon from the hand of Naomi.

10: Also, Ruth the Moabitess, the wife of Mahlon, I acquire for myself for a wife to raise up the name of the deceased in his inheritance so the name of the dead will not be cut off from the people of his tribe or from the gate of his place. You are witnesses!"

11: Then all the people who were in the gate and the elders said, "We are witnesses. May Yahweh give the woman who has come into your house to be like Rachel and like Leah, who built up, the two of them, the house of Israel, and may you do honorably in Ephrathah and may your name be famous in Bethlehem.

12: And may your house be like the house of Perez, whom Tamar bore to Judah. The seed of whom Yahweh will give to you through this woman."

13: Then Boaz took Ruth and she became for him his wife and he went in to her and Yahweh gave to her conception and she bore a son.

14: Then the women said to Naomi, "Blessed be Yahweh, who has not left you this day without a redeemer, that his name may be famous in Israel.

15: And he will be for you a restorer of life, also a provider in your old age, for your daughter-in-law has borne him; she is better to you than seven sons."

16: And Naomi took the child and laid him in her bosom and she became for him a nurse.

17: And her neighbors gave to him a name, saying, "A son is born to Naomi," and they called his name Obed. He was the father of Jesse, the father of David.

18: Therefore, these are the generations of Perez: Perez begat Hezron.

19: Hezron begat Ram and Ram begat Amminadab.

20: And Amminadab begat Nahshon and Nahshon begat Salmon.

21: And Salmon begat Boaz and Boaz begat Obed.

22: And Obed begat Jesse and Jesse begat David.

BIBLIOGRAPHY

ALTER, ROBERT. *The Art of Biblical Narrative*. New York: Basic Books, 1981.

BROWN, F., S. DRIVER, and C. BRIGGS. *The Brown-Driver-Briggs Hebrew and English Lexicon*. 9th Printing. Peabody, MA: Hendrickson Publishing, 2005.

BUSH, FREDERIC W. *Ruth. Word Biblical Commentary*. Ed. David A. Hubbard and Glenn W. Barker. Dallas: Word Books, 1996.

THE COMMISSION ON WORSHIP OF THE LUTHERAN CHURCH—MISSOURI SYNOD. *Lutheran Service Book*. St. Louis: Concordia Publishing House, 2006.

DELITZSCH, FRANZ. *Proverbs. Vol. II*. Commentaries on the Old Testament. By C. F. Keil and Franz Delitzsch. Translated by M.G. Easton. Grand Rapids, MI: William B. Eerdmans Publishing Company, 1950.

DILLARD, RAYMOND B. and TREMPER LONGMAN III. *An Introduction to the Old Testament*. Grand Rapids, MI: Zondervan, 1994.

GORMAN, MICHAEL J. *Elements of Biblical Exegesis: A Basic Guide for Students and Ministers*. Peabody, MA: Hendrickson Publishers, 2001.

HOLLADAY, WILLIAM L., ED. *A Concise Hebrew and Aramaic Lexicon of the Old Testament*. Grand Rapids, MI: William B. Eerdmans Publishing Company, 1988.

HUMMEL, HORACE D. *The Word Becoming Flesh: An Introduction to the Origin, Purpose, and Meaning of the Old Testament*. St. Louis: Concordia Publishing House, 1979.

KEIL, CARL F. *Joshua, Judges, Ruth*. Commentaries on the Old Testament. By C. F. Keil and Franz Delitzsch. Translated by James Martin. Edinburg: T. and T. Clark, 1869.

LESSING, DR. R. REED. "Psalms and Writings." Handbook for Seminary course EO–106 Spring '05–'06, Concordia Seminary, St. Louis, 2005.

LUTHER, MARTIN. *Luther's Small Catechism with Explanation*. St. Louis: Concordia Publishing House, 1986, reprint 2005.

LUTHER, MARTIN. *Lectures on Genesis: Chapters 1-5*. Luther's Works, American Edition. Vol. 1. Ed. Jaroslav Pelikan. St. Louis: Concordia Publishing House, 1960.

STEINMANN, ANDREW E. *The Oracles of God: The Old Testament Canon*. St. Louis: Concordia Academic Press, 1999.

VOELZ, JAMES W. *What Does This Mean? Principles of Biblical Interpretation in the Post–Modern World*. 2nd Edition. St. Louis: Concordia Publishing House, 2003.

WILCH, JOHN R. *Ruth. Concordia Commentary*. Ed. Christopher W. Mitchell St. Louis: Concordia Publishing House, 2006.